IN LIEU
OF FLOWERS

ALSO BY NANCY COBB

How They Met

In Lieu
of Flowers

A Conversation for the Living

Nancy Cobb

PANTHEON BOOKS NEW YORK

Library of Congress Cataloging-in-Publication Data

Cobb, Nancy.
    In lieu of flowers : a conversation for the living / Nancy
Cobb.
        p.   cm.
    ISBN 0-375-40341-8
    1. Death.   2. Death—Psychological aspects.   3. Bereavement—
Psychological aspects.   4. Grief.   I. Title.
    HQ1073.C6   2000
    306.9—dc21   99-40526   CIP

Random House Web Address: www.randomhouse.com
Book design by Johanna Roebas
Printed in the United States of America
First Edition
9 8 7 6 5 4 3 2 1

For Leland Cobb Drummond,
with eternal love

By a departing light,
We see acuter, quite,
Than by a wick that stays.
There's something in the flight
That clarifies the sight
And decks the rays.

—EMILY DICKINSON

CONTENTS

A mourner is, perforce, a person with a story. The pity is, how very rarely it gets told.

—CHRISTIAN MCEWEN

Opening the Conversation

The crossroads at the end of life—the "divine intersections" where the living meet the dying and the dying meet the dead—are difficult to discuss, perhaps because we are afraid of the unknown, perhaps because we don't want to sound morbid or New Agey. I often hear my contemporaries say, "Well, I'm not religious in the *traditional* sense, but I am *spiritual.*" I have said it myself. But if we're all so spiritual, why can't we talk about the world of the spirit? And if we're all going to die, why can't we talk about death?

Death is as sacred and inevitable, as ordinary and extraordinary, as messy and complex, as birth, and yet end-of-life care in America is only just catching up with the natural birthing methods introduced to the delivery room thirty years ago. Why, I wonder, has it taken us so long to handle our departures as lovingly as we have handled our arrivals?

Even in bookstores—from the mall behemoth to the shop around the corner—bereavement is relegated to a shelf or two in the Psychology or Self-help section, which suggests that death is either an aberrant condition or an emotional anomaly.

Conversely, the Cookbook section offers a veritable gustatory harvest, a bibliocornucopia. Shelves bulge with the most esoteric culinary information imaginable—flavors, ingredients, recipes, cultures, equipment—hundreds of volumes to tell you more than you ever needed to know about food. I could sooner learn to make a Siberian cake for a premenstrual friend on a rainy day in a high altitude than I could find solace in the weeks that followed her death if she jumped off the cliff while I baked it. (An entirely plausible plunge, by the way, given the combo of my cooking and her PMS.)

Of course, it's obvious that we all have to eat and we all have to die, just as it's obvious, given a choice, what we'd all rather do. But beyond the pop psychology—stuffing ourselves to keep the deeper feelings suppressed—I wonder what this imbalance says about our culture in general? Why is it easier to express our grief for an English princess in a French tunnel than it is to visit a dying neighbor down the block? Would that we could bring a fearlessness to a friend's deathbed or to a grieving family as easily as we now bring a casserole to an already full table on the day of the funeral.

Although there are no blueprints to guide us—no single formula, prescription, or prayer I can offer you or you can offer me—there are internal rhythms that dictate our individual responses. During the first weeks of mourning, our instincts—to stay in bed, to stare at the wall, to howl at the moon—should be respected. There is no good way or bad way to grieve, no prescribed timetable or twelve-step program to follow. Just as we die in different ways, we grieve in different ways. No matter how devastated we may be, no matter how idiosyncratic our methods of adjustment, we must deal with our grief as we see fit, in our own time frames, in response to our own needs.

My parents' deaths are my guideposts; losing them made me a bit braver about saying what needs to be said, to people who are dying, to people who are grieving, to people who are afraid to talk at all. I understand, firsthand, that there is no solace in what *might* have been said. I've learned that if I'm feeling it, I probably should be saying it. When circumstances permit, speaking from the the heart, listening and remembering, acknowledging and forgiving, will provide more long-lasting comfort than a roomful of roses.

After experiencing the death of someone you love, you join a rank-and-file whose number multiplies hourly. Soon you learn, as others have before you, that perspective shifts errati-cally. Weeks pass slowly. You wonder why the world goes on as if nothing has happened. You wonder if that bone-deep physical ache in the center of your chest will ever go away, or if you'll ever finish a paragraph, laugh with abandon, or look at family photographs without falling apart. If your loved one died suddenly you will search your memory obsessively, going over and over the last exchange of words and the predominant feelings between you that day. If you had plenty of time to say goodbye, you'll still wonder if you got it right. Regret is grief's handmaiden. Learning to focus on the life, rather than the death, of a person you have loved and lost requires an enormous emotional effort. You distract easily. You teeter constantly. Car accidents and falls down stairs often occur during periods of mourning. Because you have been cracked open by your experience, imbalance is often a result.

Just when you think you're ambulatory, it will hit again. The grief ambush can happen anywhere—the supermarket, the street corner, opening the mail, listening to the radio, watching one plump drum majorette in the St. Patrick's Day parade. The bagpipes, of course, are a real killer. A year goes by. Some people say the second is worse. Reality sinks in. Few people ask how you're doing. Grief fills the interstices. Holidays, birthdays, anniversaries; when the dog dies, when a divorce occurs, when a child leaves for college, when death dominates the headlines—a plane crash, a terrorist, a tornado. Loss has no boundaries. Grief is ongoing for all of us. How we each deal with it, though, is another matter entirely.

My father died in 1982. My mother died in 1996. I felt a primal urge to bridge these fourteen years—to reunite my parents in death as they had been united in life—by returning to the place where they were married in 1944: the Rectory of St. Patrick's Cathedral in New York.

On a frigid day in December, I walk up Forty-second Street from the train station, making a brief stop at one of my mother's favorite haunts, the New York Public Library (my father's haunts—the Turf and Field Club at Belmont, the back nine at Winged Foot, and the Oyster Bar at Grand Central— had to be saved for another day) before heading north on Fifth Avenue, past Saks, where my mother once worked as a model, and Rockefeller Center, where I scatter a round of her ashes under the feet of the trumpeting angels. This solemn deposit was the fourth of five, following the first batch flung in our woodland stream, another off a cliff at Big Sur, a third mixed through the primrose boxes at the Dickens house in London and the last, which waits in the wings for a flight to Ireland.

As I enter St. Patrick's, I spot a young priest.

"Could you direct me to the Rectory, please?" I ask.

"The Rectory?"

"The Rectory."

"I'm not familiar with the Rectory," he says. "Better try the office, Fifty-first Street entrance."

"Thanks," I say, and light a candle in the Lady Chapel, just in case.

The office is kind of a downer after the cathedral. A matched set of institutional glass doors leads to a claustrophobic waiting room across from which a woman sits—no robes, no rosaries; in fact, she may not even be a Catholic—behind a glass partition in a booth that's a dead ringer for the one at the Fifty-first Street subway stop. What the hell, I think. Give it a try. So I tell her my story by whispering it—my midday confession—into the little speaking hole. She regards me with a gimlet eye. Maybe she can tell that *I'm* not a Catholic.

"I can't help you, miss. I never heard of a Rectory around here. You'll have to speak to Father. Have a seat."

So, I have a seat. I wait. I wait some more.

Finally a middle-aged priest wends his way through two other sets of doors that resemble an airport security maze, approaches me, bows at the waist, and smiles cordially.

"Yes, dear, what can I do for you?"

I like him instantly. He is Spencer Tracy–avuncular. Plus—here's the good news—he has a brogue.

I launch into my story, making sure to tell him my mother's maiden name—McCarron, of the Donegal McCarrons—and how important it has become for me to stand in the place where my parents were married, five years before I was born.

"Well," he says slowly, "there's a bit of a problem. You see, the Rectory is no longer a rectory. It's part of the monsignor's office and, well, he's a very busy man."

"Oh, please . . . if I could just have a peek," I say. "It would mean so much. Couldn't you put in a good word for me?"

He shakes his head and smiles. "Don't count on it, dear, but I'll see what I can do."

As he walks away, I add, "Maybe I should say a little prayer to St. Christopher . . . St. Francis?"

"Try the lot of them," he says over his shoulder, laughing. "It couldn't hurt."

In fifteen minutes he's back, looking positively jubilant. He gives me two thumbs up, motions for me to follow him back through Checkpoint Charlie (the heretic blockade?), up a short flight of stairs, down a dark passageway, and through a doorway swathed in heavy velvet draperies with braided tiebacks. He ushers me into an inner sanctum, or what looks like an inner sanctum, and proceeds to open a wide wooden door with a large brass knob. He gives me a wink and extends his arm into the room as a directive.

"Good luck, dear, you're on your own now," he says, and disappears.

I round the corner and enter the monsignor's office. I have been worried about this moment. What's the appropriate protocol here? Do I curtsy? Genuflect? Kiss the monsignor's ring? The moment I lay eyes on him, however, sitting behind his enormous desk, all my tension evaporates. I can only think of one thing: *Saturday Night Live*. It's the proverbial laughing-in-church setup. This man has the blackest hair I've ever seen. He looks like John Belushi in a fright wig. I breathe deeply. I compose myself, then clear my throat.

"Thank you, Monsignor," I finally say, "for . . . uh . . . letting me interrupt your schedule. I realize how busy you must be." Then I tell him my story.

He points to a room behind me with two floor-to-ceiling windows facing Madison Avenue, the same windows, no doubt, that revealed a twilight snowfall as my parents repeated their vows on a November Saturday so many years ago. Except for the central conference table, the monsignor tells me, the room's dimensions are the same; the mouldings, the fireplace, the windows, all just as they were in 1944.

"Go," he says. "Be there. Take as much time as you need."

I enter what was once the Rectory. I stand by the windows. I imagine my parents, hand in hand, young, vital, with the promise of a long life ahead. I remain there, in silence and in tears, imagining how they looked, how they moved, how they felt about each other, knowing all the while, from my singular vantage point, of the joys and disappointments that were to follow.

"It was wartime, wasn't it?" the monsignor asks rhetorically as I turn to face him.

"It was, yes. My father was still in uniform. He was a major in the Army."

"Where was he stationed?"

"The first time in North Africa. The second, in Italy. Sicily."

The monsignor nods knowingly. "My father was born in Sicily," he says. "After he died, I too felt the need to make a pilgrimage, to visit the place of his birth."

I stand there, looking into the eyes of this man, at once a stranger and an intimate, the two of us suddenly bound in a memorial holding pattern, the monsignor with the black hair and me.

Amazingly, communal moments like this became common-place after I started writing this book. If you give yourself permission to talk about *your* experience, you'll find that other people will want to talk about *theirs*. The merest suggestion elicits a response. Faces open. Brows unfurrow. So you've been there too, the eyes say. Tell me your story. Listen to mine. Alliances are forged on the spot. These impromptu retrospectives form a kind of way station where, for a brief time, the living can connect with each other as well as reestablish their connections with the dead.

One day last year, waiting for a jitney to take me up the hill to Thomas Jefferson's home, Monticello, a security guard, an affable fellow in his sixties, asked me where I was from and what I did for a living. When I mentioned this book, his eyes suddenly brimmed with tears. His wife and son had both died of cancer within months of each other a few years back, he said, and he wanted me to know what the residual effects of each experience still meant to him.

"My son and I laughed and cried and said goodbye: we really celebrated his life . . . but my wife," he said, shaking his head sadly, "wouldn't let me in. I wanted to talk about it, but she didn't. My boy and I said what we needed to say, but I still haven't gotten over his mother's death. Painful . . . this unfinished business." He paused and cocked his head. "I bet you never had a conversation like this," he said, "with someone you don't even know."

Funny thing is, I've had many—in airports and hair salons, on commuter trains, over dinner with people I've just met or have known forever. It happens all the time. People are *dying* to talk. Maybe these conversations were run-of-the-mill once, back when we knew our neighbors and their families, lived and died in the same town, and made regular visits to the cemetery where our ancestors were buried.

These days grief seems to be as portable as everything else in our world. But if we take the time to stop and talk about it, to bring the dead to life, even momentarily, an ad hoc community takes shape, a bivouac of surprisingly comfortable proportion. Though the encampment may be temporary, the shared memories will remain. Like the dead, we will carry them with us for the rest of our lives.

IN LIEU
OF FLOWERS

Give sorrow words; the grief that does not speak whispers the o'erfraught heart, and bids it break.

—WILLIAM SHAKESPEARE

ONE

Closing the Gap

"I can't remember anything," my mother tells me in the fall of 1991. "It started with the *Times* crossword . . . I've noticed . . . writing checks, reading menus . . . I remember when I had to order for Dad, when he started to . . . Dungeness crab . . . we were in San Francisco, the summer of . . ." Her voice trails off.

"Was it 'eighty, Mom? Nineteen eighty?" I try to regain my bearings, try to establish a grid. " 'Eighty-one?"

"Around then, yes, I suppose," she says vaguely.

"You think it could have been something in that Fox Chapel Township water? Too Republican?"

She laughs. I laugh. There's our lifeline.

It was inconceivable to me, even eerie, that my mother could have Alzheimer's disease, her initial symptoms a weird reprise of my father's. How kind she had been with him in those early stages of confusion, one day carefully writing the name of my husband—Geoffrey—on a small piece of paper that my father kept folded in his breast pocket and pulled out each time he was tempted to call him Bruce.

"Bruce was my first husband, Dad. Geoffrey's the new one."

We all laughed, even my father, each of us relieved he had actually gotten the joke. But the following day he excused himself from the breakfast table, over and over again, explaining that he needed to shave.

"You shaved before breakfast, Dad, remember?" I said, stroking his cheek. The more recent the activity, it seemed, the more quickly it was forgotten.

"Oh, yes," he murmured as he mimicked my gesture, staring into space. "Before breakfast."

A scant decade later, Mark, a young and earnest gerontologist, puts my mother through a battery of tests at Yale's Dorothy Adler Geriatric Assessment Center. She tries to divert him.

"Come on, Mrs. Cobb," he persists. "Can you complete this sentence? A rolling stone _____."

She averts her eyes, waits a moment, then tries to engage him in another conversation.

"A rolling stone _____," Mark prods gently, pauses and finally finishes for her, ". . . gathers no moss."

"Oh, that's right, dammit," she says, but then brightens, adding with a sly smile, "but he has a great time on the way down."

Mark seems genuinely sad when he gives me the process-of-elimination diagnosis two weeks later.

"No organic damage indicated on the CAT scans . . .

based on the tests, her conversations, your observations . . . with your permission, I'd like to tell her."

"She knows already, Doctor. She's been marking its progress, comparing her experience with my father's, drawing parallels all along."

The following spring I decide to take my mother on what I know will be her last trip to Ithaca, New York, my father's hometown. We are heading north on the stretch of Route 17 that flanks the Beaverkill, now thaw-swollen and dotted with fishermen in glistening waders. We know this road well from trips past: family reunions at Christmastime, Cornell games in the fall when my father was alive, July's first butter-and-sugar corn from the farm stand near Hancock. On this day my own memories blur as I wonder what is going through my mother's mind.

Her voice startles me.

"Nan . . . I want you to give me a pill, to help me end my life when the time comes."

We drive in silence for several miles as my mother folds and refolds a rectangular silk scarf she has retrieved from her handbag.

"Mom . . . I'm not sure . . . I don't think I can do that."

"Of course you can." Adamant, she unfurls the scarf, draping it around her neck, fussing with the ends. "You must. I don't want to live like that. No one does."

———

As my mother's health declined, this conversation haunted me. I thought about her emphatic request, her need for control, her understandable wish for a death with dignity. I would want the same for myself.

One day, soon after I moved my mother into an apartment in the assisted-living residence near our home, I decide to address her unresolved request.

"Mom, remember when you asked me to give you a pill? To help you end your life when the time came?"

"Yes . . . I . . ." she says slowly.

"Well, that would be . . . difficult to do."

"It would?"

"Well, first of all . . ." I hesitate, then try to mask my own discomfort, "it's not as if you can take *a* pill, you know, like one Excedrin PM and it's over . . ."

At one time she would have laughed, but now she just looks blank.

"Mom, remember . . . what you said before Dad died? That when and if he were past the point . . . whatever the point was . . . and really, only the person himself can determine that point . . . you said you wanted to help him someday, because he had told you he didn't want to live like that . . . remember? . . . but you weren't sure quite how. Well . . . that's how I feel."

A long silence ensues. Finally, haltingly, my mother speaks.

"What does . . . it . . . what do you . . . mean?"

She stares at me, her expression frozen somewhere between confusion and panic. After what seems like forever, the full impact of her response sinks in; even as I write, I have the same queasy feeling I had that day. Too late . . . it's too late. The words double back on themselves. Yet, as her only child and her sole defender, I also feel a flickering of relief. How can one person be completely responsible for another's life—or death?

The woman who had asked for my help on the ride to Ithaca was no longer there. My mother, as I had known her, was disappearing. My father had been dead for a decade. I, their only child, heir to the family history, had become a near orphan overnight. Two parents. One parent. And now one who was gone by half. Our family of three demolished. Where were the witnesses? How to remember? Who would tell their stories and help me with mine? Who would resurrect a Thurber character, a Porter lyric? Name an obscure forties film star? Foxtrot around the kitchen grabbing props willy-nilly—dill eyebrows, grape earrings, carrot kazoos, the occasional lewd cucumber—no one could celebrate the absurd or skewer the sanctimonious better than my mother. My mother. The bookworm. The edgy, mercurial insomniac. The fashion plate. The ham. Stunning and funny, with all the answers. And me now, with none.

We sit together on the loveseat by her new window that overlooks a brook and a small grove of birches—the primary tree of Celtic lore—surrounded by all of her beautiful things: the silver flask collection, the Biedermeier desk, the Viennese clock, the leather-bound early editions of Dickens and Austen, the complete set of Waverly Novels and a needlepoint tapestry she completed a few years before my father's death. My mother, looking bewildered, unmoored, reaches for my hand and gives it a timid squeeze, like a frightened child desperate for reassurance.

Over the next five years a relentless erosion stripped away my mother's most basic freedoms—the ability to read, to sit still, to listen, to understand, to express herself, to enjoy a meal, a glass of wine, or a good story, until finally, only two small pleasures remained. Curiously, each one—riding in the car and dancing—required forward motion. She would ride with me anywhere, at any time, just so the car was moving, but she would only dance to Brazilian music, when, as if by magic, some dim physical sense memory took over. A slow, rhythmic side-to-side undulation inched my mother across our living room floor, until, with eyes closed and hips swaying in subtle but unmistakable sensuality, she was in a samba trance, her brief trip to freedom.

My mother and I used to have our most candid talks on long car rides, but now we travel without destination or conversation. We drive to drive and as my mother, the lifelong reader, reads the road signs, I applaud each tiny triumph.

"Rest . . . stop . . ."

"Right, Mom, that's right."

"One . . . mile."

Then, just as we begin to pass a pickup truck, she reads its black and white bumper sticker, softly at first, and then, in a louder, surer voice.

"Shit . . . happens . . . shit . . . SHIT . . . HAPPENS."

Then she looks to me for feedback.

"You got it, Mom. It sure does. It absolutely does."

Pleased, she begins to laugh. And I begin to laugh. And there again, for one fleeting moment, we recover our lifeline.

Those diminishing windows of awareness gave me false hope. They deceived me, made me believe that though my mother would never get better, she might remain there for a while, suspended in her former self, offering me the refuge of the familiar—a fleeting chiaroscuro glimpse of the woman I had known and now longed for. These reawakenings, no matter how short-lived, made it impossible for me to consider helping my mother to end her life. Even though she had actively recruited my help, who was I to presume at what point she had finally had enough?

As it turned out, I didn't have to. She decided on her own. After many days of gradually refusing to eat, in what I believe was her final act of will and determination, my mother was admitted to the Connecticut Hospice just a few miles from our home. Once she was wheeled through its double-width front door—which features a Tree of Life bas-relief hewn from its full length and width of honey-colored wood—my mother seemed to relax. Inside, a fire crackled in one of the lounge areas, artwork hung on the walls, people greeted one another in passing. This was a self-contained living community that approached the process of dying with compassion and understanding.

For nine days, my mother and our family got to know the hospice staff—almost exclusively female—and they got to know us. Like end-of-life midwives, they guided us with veteran skill, anticipating our needs, asking the right questions, advancing and retreating with delicacy and respect. I watched them counsel other families and care for one another as well. The collaborative nature of this work gave one the instant feeling of belonging. You were a part of their team, and they, of yours. Strange as it sounds, the place *did* feel like a family—and a *functional* family at that.

Peter Yarrow, whose mother died at Connecticut Hospice, comes back every year to sing to the patients and staff. How fortuitous that he should be there the same week as my mother, who had learned to love the music of Peter, Paul, and Mary through my first record album, played and replayed throughout my seventh-grade year.

Although my mother was by now in and out of consciousness, I was grateful when the nurses suggested we wheel her bed into the large central solarium—a joyful room with a glass cathedral ceiling, brick walls, and rows and rows of books—a concert habitat made to order for my mother, who now lay beside me and drifted in and out of a peaceful sleep. I, on the other hand, was a mess. A cheap weep on the best of days, I fall apart at sports events and have been known to drive-by cry—one unknown bride and groom glimpsed from my passing car and you can hang me out to dry. So imagine the effect of this particular setting: the sun flooding the room, Peter Yarrow, acoustic guitar hanging from an embroidered strap around his neck, looking pretty much the same as he always did, even without Paul and Mary, laughing and talking to the staff, the visiting families, and the patients, so vulnerable, so frail, some in wheelchairs and some in beds like my mother.

I crouch down beside her and whisper, "Mom, Peter Yarrow is going to sing. Remember, Peter, Paul, and Mary—that first album—we knew every song." My mother moves her lips as if to speak, but no sound comes out. Then Peter is singing. "Weave, weave, weave me the sunshine . . ." and I begin to cry and I can't stop. The tears I've held in all week spill out over my mother's bedclothes; I'm taken over by wracking, body-quaking sobs. I try to sing along to my mother, but I choke on the words. Music is always an emotional catalyst, but this music, folk music, skids right past my head and cracks open my heart. I cry through song after song, until suddenly

Peter is saying, "I'm going to sing one more." Panicked, a voice—actually a squeak—emerges. "Will you take a request?" I say through tears.

"Well . . . um . . . what is it?" he asks patiently, though I can tell he'd rather not. By this time I must look like a deranged raccoon, bleary-eyed, mascara run amok, but I don't care. Weakly, with all the hope in the world, I say, " 'Blowin' in the Wind'?"

He smiles. "Just what I was going to sing," he says.

We smile at each other. Then we both nod in mutual amazement, and say, simultaneously, "Synchronicity."

Honest to God.

So he starts to sing "Blowin' in the Wind" and then he walks toward me, and my mother is moving her lips again—I've got to believe she's trying to sing—until he is beside us. I trust he knows what's going on because he's been through the same thing himself in this very same place. Then he stops playing the guitar and takes my hand and takes my mother's hand, and now he's singing to us a cappella, which really gets me, and he sings the last three verses like this, with no accompaniment except the audience singing softly in the background, and in the foreground he continues to hold our hands and sing from what seems like the center of his being, binding us together into the oddest, most perfect little trio.

In a novel this would seem contrived, but I'll tell you, being there in that room filled with sunshine, with Peter

Yarrow serenading my dying mother, was, considering the circumstances, about as good as it gets.

The next day my mother awakens with a near beatific smile on her face. She stares up toward the ceiling for a long time and then turns toward me and looks into my eyes as if she is trying to penetrate my soul. Then, very slowly, she extends her delicate hand skyward and says, faintly but quite clearly, "Fog . . . and faces. See? Faces."

"It must be Dad . . ." I whisper, holding my breath.

She gestures for me to come closer and lifts her hand to caress my face, her curled fingers like gossamer across my cheek.

Again she looks into my eyes and again she smiles, her eyes now reflecting an otherworldly serenity.

"I am . . . so . . . happy," she whispers and these, her last words, hover in the air, blessing us both. At the time I thought, This is a miracle, an absolute miracle. And in retrospect I realize our time in hospice was infused with miracles, ordinary miracles, which I have come to believe are part of the spiritual energy that surrounds every death.

The night before my mother died, the eighth of her hospice stay, I was pulled back to her bedside even though I had left it only an hour before. The memory is as resonant now as it was on that cold November night three years ago.

I arrive at my mother's bedside a little after midnight. It is quiet—no radios, no visiting families—only the distant pulse of an oxygen machine.

She is asleep, her face, peaceful, illuminated by a single votive candle I have just placed on the nightstand table. A friend of mine had said to me just that morning: "In a way, your mother was your first love affair. You knew her heartbeat, her voice, her moods, her emotions . . . her eyes were the first you saw coming into this world, just as yours will be the last she sees going out of it. You are giving birth to her and to yourself as you grow to the next stage of your life."

The words float back to me like a garland of goodwill. I take my mother's hand. Our palms are pressed together as if in prayer. Stroking her fingers, one by one, each a tapered, wrinkled duplicate of my own, I lean over and barely breathe, "I love you, Mom. Dad's waiting. Give him my love. Tell him about Leland. Tell him we're fine. Tell him . . . to take you dancing."

Her eyes flutter, almost imperceptibly. She is beautiful still, skin unlined and translucent, smoothed over her fine-boned face, high brow, and cheekbones, spun silver hair fanned across the pillow. Her breathing is steady and deep. I believe she can hear me, but language seems irrelevant now, a clunky, earthbound device. I press my cheek against hers. It is surprisingly warm. I slow my own breath to correspond with hers until we are breathing together—inhale, exhale, inhale, exhale—rhythmic, elemental, as primitive and natural as labor.

We are moving together by way of the spirit, revisiting a terrain similar to the one we shared in silence for nine months so long ago.

This connection—more intuitive than mystical, more common than rare—was bred in the bone. It is, I'm convinced, deeply embedded in all of us. Had I accelerated my mother's death as she had once asked, I would have missed these nine days in hospice, which granted me an extended and tender farewell and my mother a final measure of grace. How fortunate we both were to have this last communion.

*I think we would be able to live in this
world more peaceably if our spirituality
were to come from looking not just into infinity
but very closely at the world around us—
and appreciating its depth and divinity.*

—THOMAS MOORE

TWO

Finding Your Tribe

I live in the woods on a lake a few miles north of a small town on the Connecticut shoreline founded in 1639 by—according to the commemorative sign across from Town Hall—a "band of oppressed but optimistic English puritans." Today, their plucky legacy is borne out in a central green, four war memorials, several well-preserved prerevolutionary houses, a white-spired Congregational church, a row of clapboard specialty shops, an old-fashioned hardware store, and a family-run grocery whose red-and-white-striped awning has sheltered produce for three generations.

How cozy, we thought, when our family of three moved here from New York City. Our daughter would have a more wholesome life: country air, soccer practices, bike rides to the beach, Frisbee on the Green in summer and, in winter, the annual Christmas-tree lighting heralded by carolers of all ages in a kind of harmonic Yuletide convergence. It seemed the perfect antidote to the go-for-the-burn eighties, era of junk bonds, Christian Lacroix, and the Better Baby Institute.

However, what I didn't count on was that by moving a

hundred miles northeast of New York City we had put ourselves squarely in the heart of New England, the operative
words here being square and New England. It didn't matter
that cemeteries in the area from Stonington, Connecticut, to
South Wyndham, Vermont, are loaded with my paternal fore-
bears' crumbling headstones (all of us, dead and alive, deriva-
tives of another oppressed optimist, Deacon Henry Cobb); I
realized soon after we arrived that my truest roots were not
here in New England, but there, in New York, a city I still can't
help but call home. I know, I know; it's loud, it's frantic, it's
dirty, and if you've never lived there you will never understand
why I miss the mess. But living in Connecticut made me miss
it all the more.

To this day, I long for disorder and possibility—the random encounters with sidewalk artists and street-corner phil-
osophers, the grumpy bus drivers, the ever-changing window
displays, the dog walkers, the drag queens, the merchants who
had become my friends: the Chinese tailor, the Brazilian hair
stylist, the Greek coffee-shop cousins, the Korean grocer, the
Italian shoemaker—whose father had soled Arthur Rubin-
stein's shoes, just as his grandfather had soled Toscanini's
before him—the Japanese sushi chef, and the Russian mas-
seuses, Dora and Anna, the healers of the 92nd Street Y.
I wanted to be back in my old neighborhood—with the long
established and the freshly arrived—one unpredictable poly-
glot in three square blocks.

In comparison, my present hometown, the sixth-oldest in Connecticut, feels congealed, steeped in ancestral protocol and Yankee sangfroid. This is the way we do things, it seems to say. Don't get too close, don't make a fuss, don't talk too loud. Any expression of emotion short of a sigh could be deemed histrionic.

Luckily, I have found a couple of friends who talk as fast as I do and feel similarly at sea in the checkout line at the Big Y. Still, I'm always on the lookout for other rebellious forces, for critical mass, for one or two more tribe members easily recognized for a certain look in the eye: equal parts lively and irreverent. Last fall, in my bank, of all places—my bank that doesn't look like a bank because it's housed in a landmark saltbox surrounded by a thigh-high picket fence and features a Betsy Ross interior with American eagle accents and primary Pilgrim colors: putty green, ghastly gold, and icky ochre—I spotted a young recruit, just south of the Seth Thomas clock.

I approached this woman—a new employee, I surmised—her tumble of curls and open face a welcome contrast to the automatic-teller smile. As I pushed my check toward her, I remembered I wanted a record of it, to hang on my office wall, and asked her if she could make me a quick copy. It was a payment that had arrived—on my mother's birthday—from the *New York Times* for an essay about my parents' deaths.

"You're a writer?" she asked. "What do you write about?"

"Only love and death," I replied.

She laughed, then took a long pause and leaned in conspiratorially. "My grandmother died last year," she said, lowering her voice. "I miss her so much. We were very close."

"Has she come to you in any way?" I asked. "I mean, since her death?"

She stared at me for a moment, open-mouthed.

"Yes, she has . . . but . . ." she said, glancing furtively over each shoulder, "I don't talk about it very often . . . people think you're . . . you know . . . crazy."

"I don't think you're crazy," I said. "These things happen all the time."

"My sisters have seen her too. But . . . we're Italian . . ."

"Hey, the spirit world's equal-opportunity . . ."

She laughed again. More proof. Definitely not a Pilgrim.

By now I'm aware of a growing group-eavesdrop as some of the other tellers lean into our conversation.

"My grandmother lived with us when we were kids," she confided, unaware of her neighbors' interest. "We were as close to her as we were to our parents. Sometimes closer. About a week after she died, she came to me in a dream—or I think it was a dream—it woke me up . . . it felt like she was right there in the room. She told me she was really very happy. She looked so beautiful, so peaceful, you know?"

"It must have been reassuring," I said, "to see her like that."

"Oh, it was. I took it as a sign . . . a good omen. The next day I called my sister to tell her about the dream—she lives in the next town—and she had the exact same dream. Can you believe that?"

"Yes," I said, nodding, "I can."

When I saw the teller a week later—don't you love that, the *teller*—I told her about my own experience. A few days after my mother's death I was folding laundry in our living room, mechanically sorting through a pile of my daughter's T-shirts and jeans, gazing at a makeshift altar on the credenza—a triptych of Florentine angels illuminated by a votive candle that I would light every evening in my mother's memory. I was alone in the house. Suddenly, I sensed my mother's presence. I looked around and then spoke as matter-of-factly as if she were there helping me sort and fold, "Mom, I believe that you're here—I mean I can feel it." I paused, feeling a little odd but at the same time remembering the stories I'd heard about spirits and light, particularly candlelight.

"Look, if you are here, Mom—no pressure or anything— but could you give me some kind of a sign? You know, maybe do something with the candle?" and as soon as the words were out of my mouth, the flame began to flutter and twist, to elongate, flatten out, bob and weave wildly. It was strange and not strange. I thought for a minute that it must be a blast of heat or a draft or something other than what it must have been: my mother reassuring me that she was around in some form now filtering through a new, albeit hard-to-define, channel.

I believe the dead linger and that the weeks that follow a death are the time to pay close attention and to be open to the possibility of their presence. Other times they make an "appearance" after months or even years. It is crucial to remember that their spirit may be manifested in a variety of forms and will not necessarily respond to a direct request, like mine, or be as obviously "there" as my mother seemed to be in that moment.

For instance, my friend Susie heard her younger brother, who had died days earlier, calling her name in the night. The next morning when she told her older brother what had happened, he was dumbfounded. At the same hour in another part of the house, he too had heard their brother calling his name.

Another friend told me that while she was nursing her newborn daughter, her great-aunt appeared before her as an apparition, smiling, as if to welcome the baby into the world. And, as it turns out, this baby, who is now sixteen, is remarkably like that aunt in disposition and creativity. Her mother, who cannot "sew a stitch," is astonished by her daughter's ability to make elaborate patterns and sew her own clothes; the aunt, the child's namesake, had been a dress designer.

My friend Barbara's younger brother John died in a car accident when he was twenty-one. Skidding off a rain-slicked Iowa road, his day-old Porsche, a graduation present from his father, hit a telephone pole. John was killed instantly, his right eye and brain pierced by the turn signal. Two years later Barbara and her friend David—who looked quite like her brother, played the same brand of twelve-string guitar, and shared an equivalent passion for Leo Kottke—simultaneously watched John "walk" through the doorway and into the living room where they had been working on a song, "in a halo of white light, smiling broadly, and carrying his guitar." In the same moment David's right eye—and his right eye *alone*—began to overflow with tears. Barbara said she took this appearance as a sign from her brother of both his well-being and his wish for peace in her own life.

Six months after the death of her eighty-year-old husband, my friend Judith returned to their beloved summer house in Vermont, with its views of the Green Mountains and Caspian Lake. She spent her first day back gardening and putting the house in order. She had asked her grandniece to spend the night, and they lingered over dinner reminiscing about summers past. Near midnight, about an hour after her niece had retired, Judith went upstairs. She had been in bed only a few moments when she was startled to see a "golden light" flooding the area in front of the house. At first she thought it might be the headlights of a car but there was nothing approaching. The light somehow emanated from the house, but she checked and all the lights had been turned off. There was no explanation. The pool of light simply hung there, illuminating the immediate landscape. And then after two or three minutes it disappeared as suddenly as it had appeared.

Another friend John, a twenty-nine-year-old actor now

living in Los Angeles, was born and raised in St. Louis by his father and his grandparents. His mother died of cancer when he was ten. Seven years later, on the eve of his departure for college, John's mother came to him in a dream, a dream that he says "did not really feel like a dream at all."

"It was as if I wasn't really asleep," John recalls. "I had been anxious all week, about leaving home and going from a private school with small classes to the University of Texas, which had sixty thousand students. In the middle of the night, my mother appeared—materialized—at the foot of my bed in a kind of angelic light—floating, ethereal, looking a little like Glinda, the Good Witch in *The Wizard of Oz*. She told me not to worry, that I was going to be fine and that she was very proud of me. I 'awoke' with a start, in a flood of tears, although I wasn't sad, really; I was filled with this overall body energy: joy. This was the connection I had always hoped and prayed for from the day she died. It had a massive calming effect. My mother was watching over me and I had the same safe feeling I had experienced when she held me as a little boy. She said, 'I believe in you, I am here for you. I'll look after you.' It's what every child wants from their parents."

Mentioning how many people I have met who have "sensed" the presence of the dead prompted my teller to talk about the previous weekend when, depressed and wrestling with a difficult family issue, she recognized a fragrance reminiscent of her grandmother in a local store, an incident she regarded as another good omen, even "if it was someone else's perfume." The following day her family dilemma was resolved, a solution she attributed to her grandmother's divine, if aromatic, intervention.

My teller and I—and all the people I've talked to before and since—discovered a common link. Enlivened, ironically, by death, we were, in short, in synch. Simply put, we had something in common, and having discussed it personally, despite the impersonal setting, had reinforced the fact that our own experiences may not have been as unorthodox as we had originally thought.

Not so long ago—back when we communicated in three dimensions, when we were born in the bedroom and "laid out" in the parlor, when rituals occurred under the same roof and connected generations—life support happened at home. Folk wisdom about teething babies, arthritic knees, wedding toasts, and funeral arrangements was dispensed with a matter-of-factness now reserved for voice mail, an accurate term indeed for the bland, rote messages we leave today.

Once upon a time, at holiday gatherings, cherished family stories were taken out, dusted off, and retold year after year until they took on a patina impossible to duplicate on the ever present videotape, which will never vary, no matter how many times it is replayed.

These days, slaves to the lens and the screen, we chronicle rather than experience, observe rather than engage. Our images are diffused by flattened-out intermediaries—*terminals*—and distortion is often the result, a distortion that invariably produces an arm's-length view of life and, in turn, of death. The farther we get from the source, the smaller the picture becomes. As we lose our sense of community, it's no wonder we view the end of life, whether sudden or protracted, with surprise, as if we believed all along that every reel came with a never-ending supply of tape.

Truth is—not the sad truth, just the truth—no one's getting out of here alive, no matter how big their house is. If we can't accept that, we're bound to feel betrayed by the denouement. Rather than waiting for the last act, wouldn't it be wiser to pay attention to performance along the way—to the work we choose, the place we call home, the people we love?

Perhaps the ultimate payoff for a life lived consciously is a death faced with more acceptance than regret. But consciousness requires vigilance. In a world that extols the external, intuition can be easily dismissed. If only in hindsight we realize we should have heeded that inner voice—the one that told us not to marry as the wedding day approached, not to remain in that dead-end job, not to move to the place where we felt ill at ease—it is too late.

Finding my tribe has helped to keep me on course. When

I get smug about my station in life, they tell me exactly where to get off. Of course, I've been forced to reorganize my member list once or twice, but hey, who hasn't? As my friend Judy used to say, "Just make sure you can count on them in the revolution. That's when you know they're for real."

A wisdom as constant as the North Star shines within all of us. It is always present, waiting to be tapped, waiting to guide us, to advise us. We need only use it to prevent its atrophy. No matter what our background, profession, color, or religion, employing this universal compass, this innate sense of what we know to be true, will help us establish a lifelong foundation—a place we can go to recover our sanity and to regain our balance.

My bank teller reinforced this belief for me. Her story is only one of many. If you pay attention, you too will discover people like her, people whose openness will assure you that tribe members can crop up just about anywhere. Even in New England.

We are not human beings on a spiritual path, but spiritual beings on a human path.

—JEAN SHINODA BOLEN

THREE

Unexpected Connections

My father and all but one of his three siblings were conceived in Blue Grass country and born in Ithaca, nine months later, under the sign of Cancer. My grandfather, an entrepreneurial attorney who died before I was born, invested in all kinds of things, from a railroad in Virginia to a filly named Miss Adbell, who won the final leg of the trotting's Triple Crown, the Kentucky Futurity, in 1905.

Gambling was in the Cobb blood. As a result, my childhood memories of family vacations will be forever linked to horse-racing. There was Lake George (and Saratoga) in the summer, Key Biscayne (and Hialeah) in the winter, and New York on spring and fall weekends (Aqueduct and Belmont). By the time I was ten I had been to every major racetrack on the East Coast. Unfortunately, my favorite, Delaware Park, which I thought looked exactly like Tara, was off-limits to children. Because of the state's Blue Laws I had to be smuggled in— patent leather Mary Janes skittering along under the plaid lining of my father's Burberry—past the averted eye and greased palm of a green-uniformed track official. When we were safe inside the air-conditioned clubhouse, my mother would order eggs Benedict and I would order multiple Shirley Temples from waiters in jackets with gold buttons and epaulets, as my father handicapped the horses, a methodical process that entailed scribbling all over "The Morning Telegraph," "The Scratch Sheet," and the day's program listings, until the mass of barely decipherable print—the odds, track conditions, horses' lineages and past performances—produced his projected winner. I, however, preferred cute jockeys in purple silks on horses with even numbers. Although my father would patiently attempt to parse out the variables for me, it was he, on the rare occasion when my long shot did come through, who most delighted in my success.

Sitting at a table adorned with starched napery and a basket of fresh flowers, far above the stub-littered grandstand, made it easy for my father to rationalize his lifelong habit. "Wall Street," he would say, "is a bigger crap shoot than this."

When the man in the red cutaway trumpeted the horses' arrival on the track, my mother would look at my father seductively and say, "Listen, darling, they're playing our song." He would always chuckle, she would always reach for his hand, or stroke the back of his neck, and then she'd turn to me and say, "Your father has the most beautifully shaped head," as if she were describing the day's odds-on favorite.

But as the years passed, his addiction became the central theme of their ongoing battles and as a result I have never, nor will I ever, buy so much as a lottery ticket. It's one habit I can live without.

My father's only nongambling and last surviving sibling still lives in Ithaca, in a rambling grey Victorian in the middle of a town filled with memories that remain the best of my father's gifts to me.

"Tell me a story about the olden days, Daddy," I'd say, and he'd summon up one of a well-polished handful, worth the retelling for the characters alone: Fred (can't-drive-a-spike-with-a-tackhammer) Payne, oracle of the Ithaca Icewagon; Gil Dobie, the Cornell football coach; Tarby Tarbell, my father's accomplice in the foiled Hershey Bar heist near Cascadilla Creek, a cautionary tale of purloined chocolate and consequences of excess.

My favorite story transpired a decade later, when Mr. J. Edgar Pew (always Mr.) offered my father a post-college job as a roustabout in the oil fields of West Texas. On his first morning in a Dallas hotel, a little old lady corralled my very tall father in the lobby and implored him to meet her tour group from the East—"to show them what a real Texan looked like."

"Why sure ma'am," he obliged, in his best Ithaca drawl, "I'd be happy to."

My father was a natural storyteller and I, his most faithful audience. The hours we logged together—his talking and my listening—are, no doubt, the key to my fascination with other people's stories, which are the foundation of my work.

Two years after my father's death, I returned to Ithaca with my own little girl, to visit my aunt in the house on Tioga Street, the house with the windowed pantry filled with floor to ceiling glass-fronted cabinets which display a mix of my grandmother's Limoges and crystal, my aunt's pottery and olivewood bowls. The blur of past and present has not changed the smell or the feel of this space, its slightly musty odor, a familiar comfort still. In one olfactory instant I can conjure my ten-year-old self, sliding a chubby hand into the Home Dairy Bakery box with the slack red string, in search of one more saucer-sized sugar cookie—my own childhood momentarily sandwiched between my father's and my daughter's.

This house will probably be sold long before my child, now a teenager, has stories to tell to her own children. There is a connection, however, beyond birthright, that binds her to this place in a kind of trust established in the autumn of 1984.

I had spent that October day with my aunt and my mother, polishing silver, listening to stories about my grandparent's parents as my daughter played at our feet. My aunt, a child psychologist, and my mother were always examining the underpinnings of people's lives, focusing on behavior related to long-standing family patterns.

My grandmother's unkindness, for instance, was the result

of repressed grief over three deaths: her parents, before she was twelve, and her firstborn child. I don't recall ever seeing her smile. She was critical of everything and everyone. Table manners, posture, diction, wardrobe. My aunt, her mother's staunchest defender, often reminded us that my grandmother suffered from accumulated sorrow, bottled up since childhood and cloaked in intellect and intolerance as she grew older. She was never able to grieve fully or mourn the amassed losses, my aunt had said. If we repress our grief, over time, it's bound to harden the heart.

I was restless that night and read for a long time before turning out the light, kissing my daughter, and snuggling up beside her in the same four-poster cherry bed my father had slept in as a boy.

Suddenly, I was aware that someone, or something, was with us. What was this feeling, this swirl of energy around me? The bed began to vibrate as if it had a pulse of its own. A palpable presence seemed to be moving through the room.

I sat up and scanned my surroundings for a visible clue, though I'm not sure what I expected to see. A cloud of vapor? A smoky wisp? The brush and hand mirror floating off the dresser?

Then, with no warning, it stopped as abruptly as it had started. Departed. Just like that. The bed was still. The chill was gone. An eerie quiet remained.

I had seen nothing, but I had absolutely felt, had absolutely sensed, something. I will swear to that. I was awake, alert, observant. This was not a dream. But still I thought, Be logical. Was it the wind? No open windows. My mother? Asleep in the next room. An earthquake? Unlikely in these parts. Was this a disgruntled ghost? A passing spirit? My father? My grand-mother, unsettled by our conversation that day?

I gave in to an absurd urge to wake my daughter and query her in all her infant wisdom.

"Did you feel that?" I asked, giving her a small nudge. "What was it?" Oblivious, she slept on, my only potential wit-ness, inert. (A friend later told me that small children and ani-mals are often conduits for the spirit world, because their "beings are more pure and less congested" than ours.)

Early the next morning I crossed the short hallway that connected my room to my mother's. She was sitting up in bed, reading, as usual.

"Mom." I hesitated. "Last night . . . did you feel a . . ."

She finished my sentence.

"Around one-thirty, two? Something, someone . . . I felt it."

"Remember . . . the four-poster? Do you think it could have been . . . Dad?"

She was quiet for a while.

"I don't think so . . ." she said slowly, and added after a long pause, "He would have asked about the Super Bowl."

For as long as I can remember, my mother and I communicated in a kind of psychic shorthand, often laced with hilarity, that I can neither explain nor corroborate. My mother viewed the world through an intuitive lens. An infallible analyst of nuance, she could predict a stranger's character by simply observing a look or a gesture. She foretold the future with spooky accuracy.

The day before the *Challenger* accident she called me with a dire warning.

"They are making a mistake," she had said. "I know it. I just know it. It sounds ridiculous, but I feel like calling NASA."

Too bad she didn't. I still regret a couple of instances when I didn't adhere to her warnings, tamping down my own latent instinct out of stubborn rebellion. To her credit she never called me on it, allowing me to find my own way.

It was not until my mother was diagnosed with Alzheimer's disease, however, that this lens became fully operative in me. As she lost language, I began to depend on our intuitive connection and found myself translating for her with increasing frequency the thoughts and fears I tried to read in her face, the intermittent relief in her eyes the only reassurance I was getting it right.

Once, in trying to describe a dream, she acted it out, charades-style, turning in half circles, pointing ahead of her and behind her. "You were back there," she said, gesturing over her shoulder. "That way." Eventually, I realized she was talking about my childhood.

Alzheimer's disease is a slow-motion race run in reverse, its course unalterable. Just as the patient's caregivers become accustomed to a new failing, another appears. Initial forgetfulness and disorientation give way to aggression and paranoia. Depression and disinhibition are common at first and then gradually disappear. A compulsive repetition of tasks demarcates an Alzheimer's patient's day—in my mother's case, opening and closing her pocketbook, folding and unfolding paper napkins, stashing books in her oven and money in her freezer, cutting out pictures of the basketball coach Pat Riley from the sports page, as well as editorials she no longer understood, from her lifelong habit, the *New York Times*.

Thus, for the patient's family, mourning begins long before the Alzheimer's patient dies. "Reappearances" of the person diminish over time. The frisson of a former self, an occasional flash of humor, one quickly discovers, is as ephemeral as a firefly's glow at summer's end. Unlike other diseases, where in spite of the infirmity it is possible to communicate to the last, Alzheimer's disease forces us into a premature lament for a person who is locked away in a distant place and unable to return.

A friend of mine was a prisoner of war for seven years in Vietnam in a hell euphemistically called the Hanoi Hilton. He lived in unspeakable conditions, seldom seeing the light of day and, beyond his captors' beatings, rarely feeling the touch of another human hand. He says that the days were interminable but the years flew by. Robbed of his most elemental freedoms, he survived by retreating into the world of his imagination, the one thing they could not take from him. This Air Force pilot was able to circumnavigate the globe, savor a steaming bowl of his mother's soup, build a working farm from the ground up, teach himself French via code tapped on his cell wall by a neighboring prisoner, and reconstruct thousands of lines from poems he never knew he had learned. Understandably he almost never speaks of these years. The rest of us, barely able to fathom such deprivation and cruelty, can only respect his need for privacy by honoring his heroism from a distance.

Though I would never presume to liken his experience to my mother's, I have often thought of the irony inherent in their comparison. His mind—his salvation and only source of light—was her prison, the seat of her ever-darkening universe.

After five years my mother still recognized us, but the dullness in her eyes, her loss of appetite, her inability to enjoy anything, even her granddaughter, fashioned a trap she could not even comprehend. Captive to a fragmented mind and an increasingly frail body, she was constantly restless, jumping up randomly and heading for the nearest door, as if trying to outrun some demon force. She could manage only a few steps before she would stumble and fall. My once-elegant mother would have been appalled to see herself—one of a dozen ill-clad denizens in the ersatz Colonial dining room of an assisted-living wing—and me, the dutiful daughter trying to coax her into one more spoonful of applesauce. Her inability to name it, my inability to change it, became a Möbius strip of frustration, a tandem curse.

"Come on, Mom," I remember saying on a Sunday afternoon, "just one bite . . ."

All of a sudden, out of nowhere, her listlessness gives way to fury. She glares at the plate, glares at me, and then raises her chin in defiance, and in that moment, my mother, as if fully possessed by her former self, reappears long enough for me to understand the deliberateness and the desperation behind her gesture. I've had it, her eyes say. I hate this place. Get me out of here.

I sit there, looking at my mother, and perhaps for the first time in months really see her. Had my need to nurture become a slow form of torture? Had my idea of sustenance been a way to protect myself, to blanket my own anxiety?

I stand up. I take my mother's hands and help her out of the pastel Naugahyde chair on wheels. We turn and walk out of the dining room arm in arm. Everyone is silent. We round the corner and begin the awkward push-me-pull-you shuffle along the carpeted corridor. I back down the hall and ease her along, slowly, whispering encouragement, guiding her baby steps as she once guided mine. She stops periodically, looks into my eyes, regains her bearings, then stares down at her black Chinese slippers, as if her feet belonged to someone else.

Back in her apartment I begin to undress her. She fumbles with one button and mumbles incoherently. I kiss her and explain each task in a soothing voice.

"Lift your arms, Mom."

She stares at me, bemused. Her arms hang lifeless at her sides.

I smooth lotion on her hands, wash her face, brush her teeth, slip a long cotton nightgown over her head. This role reversal started two years earlier when, her arms outstretched and beseeching, she began to call me "Mother" whenever she saw my face.

"You used to do this, Mom, tuck me in at night, sing 'Sweet and Low.' Remember?"

"Okay," she says faintly. "Okay."

I lead her like a sleepwalker to the bed, pull back the covers, fluff up her pillow, and help her slide her bony frame into a comfortable position.

She looks lost. Her expression alternates between pleading and detachment; her eyes, vacant; her lower lip, trembling. I sit on the edge of her bed, stroke the skein of spidery veins on the back of her hand, and begin to sing the lullaby she once sang to me:

"Sweet and low. Sweet and low. Wind of the western
   seas.
Low, low, breeze and blow, wind of the western
   seas.
Over the rolling waters flow, come to the dying moon
   and blow,
Blow him again to me, while my little one,
While my pretty one sleeps . . ."

I stop. There's a lump in my throat. I am a little girl again, listening to her mellow contralto, wondering, What is a dying moon, anyway? The song kindles something in my mother; her eyes are filled with tears.

"Mom," I say, my voice barely a whisper. "Oh, Mom . . . I think you are trying to die. I think you've been trying to tell me this . . . and . . . if you want to, if you're ready, it's okay to go. Dad will be waiting. It's time, don't you think?"

At this point my voice cracks. I have finally uttered something I believe we both have known for some time.

"Do you understand, Mom? I will be safe; we will all be safe. And you . . . will be . . . free . . ."

My mother's face slowly begins to change, to brighten, as if illuminated by some internal beacon. Age falls away. Her eyes soften. And then, my mother does the most astonishing, miraculous thing. She raises her hands to my face, and tenderly, purposefully, traces first my brow, then my cheeks, my nose, my lips with her fingertips, as if trying to commit my face to memory—for eternity—and communicate to me, on the deepest level, that she understands what I have said. Her gaze, her touch, tell me everything I need to know.

Ring the bells that still can ring
Forget your perfect offering.
There is a crack in everything
That's how the light gets in.

—LEONARD COHEN

FOUR

In Memory

I never suffered from prepartum jitters or postpartum blues, but rather experienced a heady sense of well-being before and after my daughter's birth. Perhaps because the upcoming excursion required complete surrender, it was the only time in my life I was totally relaxed. I figured that control, or more accurately, the illusion of control, was a ludicrous concept in this arena. Consequently, as delivery day approached, I awaited its outcome with more curiosity than trepidation.

One piece of advice, though: if you go into labor in New York City, do not hail a taxi in plain view. I learned, the hard way, that most cabbies do not take kindly to very pregnant women. When they see one, they think, Possibly litigious, probably messy, pretend you don't see her. So, put your partner in the front line and keep your belly out of sight. I eventually crouched between the front and rear bumpers of two closely parked cars on the corner of Lexington and Ninety-third and pushed against them during contractions. When my husband finally secured a cab and I emerged from my curbside hideout, he wedged me into the backseat of what was definitely not a Checker: the seat was caved in, the radio was blaring, and the cab reeked of the cigar the driver was smoking. On my very best day, cigar smoke—whether it emanates from a dime-store stogie or a turbo Havana (the *ne plus ultra* in penis substitutes)—makes me retch. As a result, I spent the sixteen-block ride to Lenox Hill Hospital panting like a cocker spaniel with my head hanging out the back window. When we got out of the cab, the driver said in a monotone, "Have a good night," without even looking up. Believe it or not, the guy didn't even notice I was pregnant. As fate would have it, though, seventy-two hours later, his benevolent counterpart, Mr. Rodriguez, gave our new family a ride home and refused to take a dime. Just another one of those glorious New York contradictions that makes me miss the sidewalks.

Back at home, postpartum, I realized that, aside from a few transportation tips, no one should give you bottom-line advice on how to give birth to your child, any more than anyone should tell you how to help your mother to die. People can recount their experiences—that is, what worked for them—but you must remember to take in the information as a suggestion, not as a foregone conclusion. Try it on for size. See what works for you.

Take Lamaze, for instance. They give you their spiel-in-stone: puff-puff-blow, breathe your way to natural childbirth. A dozen mothers-to-be and their partner guides flop around on the floor until they feel sure that this final postfertility drill has fully prepped them for the big event. This is what you must do to have a baby, they say. My husband and I, being the compulsive students that we are, committed our orders to memory. But what they didn't mention, and what we didn't consider, is variety. Individual circadian rhythms. Differences in style, in approach, and in pelvis.

For starters, what happens if you're a blow-puff-puffer? Or a blow-puff-blower? You're stuck with the wrong birth routine and you're working twice as hard to overcome your own instincts in order to subscribe to someone else's tidy credo.

Our Lamaze instructor, for instance, glossed over information on back labor—"it's extremely painful, but don't worry, only one in twenty births is a back labor."

Naturally, I, the one in twenty, was sorely unprepared for this natal variation and went through several trial-and-error positions before I discovered one that worked, though I use that verb advisedly. My breathing techniques, which evolved from nine months of swimming the aptly named crawl, were completely unorthodox: arrhythmic, off-the-charts. Actually, I thought breathing—period—was an accomplishment. My husband rubbed my back through the last hours of labor, once he realized that it was okay to discontinue timing the contractions on his special father chart. (It's important to give the men concrete assignments when the women are otherwise engaged.)

Still, I toughed it out and just said no to drugs, which in retrospect was pretty dumb. I think my oppressed optimist genes must have kicked in during the fight-or-flight portion of the trip. When my daughter finally slid into the world on her actual "due" date—the only one in our family, ever, to be on time—all I could do was smile. Smile and cry and marvel, with my husband, over the most original and extraordinary event in our lives. I felt as if I were the first mother, the earth mother, the only mother, ever. This natural high was followed by lactation nirvana and, in spite of our drug-free delivery, my daughter and I were one blissed-out first-time team.

The local New York merchants—the group I mentioned earlier—who had watched my ballooning waistline now welcomed our baby to the block, taking a kind of territorial pride in her arrival. Nestled in her Snugli, she traveled with me everywhere—even when she was a month old, to California, where my husband had some business and I had an old friend, Jayne. I had known Jayne forever—since I was six and she was seven and our fathers worked for the Sun Oil Company in Pittsburgh.

I suggested we meet at the Tadich Grill, a San Francisco landmark with a block-long mahogany bar, tiled floors, and paneled walls that had been a favorite of my dad's over the years. It seemed as though nothing had changed since it opened its doors in 1849 as "The Original Cold Day Restaurant," including the entrees, which were baked, boiled, or fried. (As opposed to infused, sun-dried, or truffled.) Their menu featured comfort food: calf's liver, beef brisket, Pacific oyster stew, and for a grand lumpy finale, rice pudding with raisins— in the era of dessert as architecture, a humble deconstructionist treat.

Though there weren't any other mothers with newborns in tow, this vintage watering hole was appropriately nostalgic for a long afternoon of memories with my childhood friend. Fortunately the waiters, who looked as homespun as the menu, left us alone in our reverie.

Though happy to introduce Jayne to the newest member of our family, I was also sad to have to tell her that my father had some form of dementia.

"My parents thought of San Francisco as a second home," I told her, "and now my father will never be back."

It felt just right, though, being in the city that my father so loved, with his first grandchild. He would have been pleased to see that we had chosen Tadich's, over, say, Grace Cathedral. For him, their oyster stew was a religious experience.

The week before we left I had been shocked by my dad's appearance. When he and my mother arrived in New York for a visit, he was disoriented and fretful. He paced constantly, asking the same question over and over again—"Where is that guy?"—whenever my mother was out of sight. Even his eagerly anticipated grandchild was a mystery to him, and when I told him we were taking her to San Francisco, he looked at me for a long while before asking, "Where is that?"

In six short months my father had deteriorated so rapidly that my mother confided to me her dread of what was to come. We discussed health care options. Round-the-clock nursing? She worried about his size: six feet five. How will we handle him if he becomes belligerent or physically incapacitated? He loathed the idea of a nursing home and vowed years earlier that he would sooner "do himself in than go through that." At one point three days into their stay, my mother later told me, he looked out the window of our eleventh-floor apartment and said with unusual clarity, "I can't take it anymore. Sometimes I feel like jumping."

On the day our new family of three left for California, my father escorted us out to a waiting cab. In spite of his memory loss, my ever-courtly father retained a sense of decorum. He helped the driver with our bags, opened the taxi door, and after our long embrace, he saluted my husband with a wink and a nod. As we pulled away, my father—still so handsome, so tall—stood under the canopy of our building grasping its brass pole, as if trying to anchor himself in a rapidly shifting terrain. I waved back, tears welling up as I watched my father grow smaller and smaller through the rear window of the cab, until he vanished from sight.

———

My memory of what happened two weeks later is as clear today as it was on that November morning fifteen years ago:

We are back in our New York apartment, having just flown in the night before from our two-week California sojourn. The phone rings and startles all three of us out of a jet-lagged sleep. My husband answers. His face goes slack. He grips the receiver with one hand and my arm with the other. "What?" I plead. "What is it?"

He listens briefly and then hands me the phone, our daughter crying between us. My mother's voice is hollow on the other end.

"Nan," she says, "Dad is dead . . ." and my own voice over hers, "Oh God, how, when . . . ?" I begin to shake uncontrollably. As she goes over the details, I sit, stunned, unable to stop the shaking, taking in what I can, imagining his last moments.

After I hang up the phone, the three of us cling to each other on the bed until the baby, picking up on our anxiety, lets out a high-pitched wail. As my husband and I talk over the details of what actually happened, I realize that my father has been dead since Monday. Monday? It is now Thursday. For three days I didn't even know that my father was dead. The very day I was in California with Jayne, my father was in Florida preparing to jump from the balcony of their apartment to the pavement eighteen floors below.

I could not square these two events in my mind. How could I have been laughing? Talking over the good times, the old days. How could I have not sensed that something was amiss? How could I have not known my father was about to die? I remember his face as he waved goodbye, the last time I saw him alive.

It was now Thursday morning. My mother had waited until we were back home to tell me, assuming it would be the most thoughtful course of action. But knowing my father had died three days earlier complicated my anguish. I was his only child and I was the last in the family to find out. I felt betrayed. My mother thought she was doing the best thing by not telling me, because we were away from home, because of the new baby, but, as is usually the case, telling the truth would have been better than withholding it. At least for me.

I went off to the Y in a daze. It was the first time I had been there since giving birth six weeks earlier. The 92nd Street Y was my neighborhood refuge, the place where I swam through my pregnancy, the place where I discovered Dora, the Russian masseuse, reader of aches, and palms, and auras. When she saw me that morning, she knew instantly that something was wrong and embraced me without a word. Something about Dora, some all-knowing fusion of ancient and mystic, defined security.

I swam laps mechanically. The cool water, the smell of chlorine, the faraway sound of children's laughter in the showers, echoed my feelings of being in a dream. My father was dead. How could that be?

With each rhythmic stroke I am propelled backward, into

my childhood, into a run-together memory of my father . . .
teaching me to swim . . . to field a ball, choke up on the bat . . .
choose a 2-iron, no, a wood . . . playing chess, Christmas
morning, my mother reads . . . winter, summer, the Pirates . . .
the players float by, flat black numbers on lean striped backs.
Number 7 . . . Stuart . . . clowning, Smoky . . . 6, catching,
Virdon third, Dick Groat, Don Hoak . . . right field, Cle-
mente . . . *arriba*, Roberto . . . he died in a plane crash after the
Series . . . we beat the Yankees . . . the fans went wild . . . we
were there in Forbes Field and we cheered and we cheered
from our seats near the dugout as the ball sailed over the left-
field wall . . . Maz circled the bases, leaped over the bases . . .
years later my mother said, "You wore your dad's fedora" . . .
and he said, "It was a hat, Helen, just a hat."

In the steam room, as my thoughts continue to careen
around my brain, half-crazed and haphazard, the past and the
present collide. Surrounded by bodies, folds of flesh draped
over tiled risers, dim outlines in thick fog, I begin to imagine
my father, my father falling, flailing, plummeting.

I close my eyes. I piece together my father's last moments.
His determined walk from the den through the living room to
the balcony door, which he opens and closes in one fluid, silent
movement. Far below, sea breezes rustle the palm trees, the
reflection of a full moon spills across the Atlantic, and several
boats motor northward on the Intracoastal Waterway, some
strung festively with early holiday lights. But my father sees
none of this, or all of this, as he drags a wrought-iron chair to

the balcony rail and hoists his long frame onto its faded cushion. Teetering, he steadies himself in air as humid as a ceremonial bath. He stares out at the inky horizon, then pushes himself up and over and tumbles down into the night sky.

I realized that my father's death was like his life: aggressive and dignified. He was an athlete, a war hero, an executive, a gambler. Shuffling glassy-eyed down some nursing-home corridor would not have been his style. For my father, suicide became the only possible option. We had no weapons, he was beyond understanding pills, and Dr. Kevorkian's macabre carnival would have appalled him. This was his way. And maybe in taking his own life, my father somehow believed he was saving ours.

What I didn't realize, though, was how crucial it is to say goodbye, which is impossible when death is unexpected. Perhaps that is why I was compelled to reconstruct and ritualize his death in my mind, to create a rational and compassionate context, a more humane environment for an act that was violent and solitary and abrupt.

I have come to learn that this desire to make sense of the chaos is a natural part of healing. It will take some of us longer than others to find a balance and move on. We must guard our own internal responses, trust our own sense of things, and allow the process, like birth, to guide us.

Months after my father's death I would find myself overcome with a sudden rush of grief. The memory of his funeral. The satiny grain of his walnut coffin. The black folds of the minister's robe, illuminated by a single ray of sun. My newborn daughter's breath, warm in the crook of my neck, and the strange hum, melodic and melancholy, she sustained through the reading of the Twenty-third Psalm. In retrospect, I understand this series of pictures to be an integral part of my lament. Sixteen years later the aroma of roasting chestnuts, early morning light on a baseball diamond, a distant train whistle—the simplest things still catch me off guard. I stop to catch my breath, awash in the memory of my father and my own sense of loss. A few months ago I was hit with a wave of regret at my daughter's soccer game when she sailed a powerful kick into the net with those never-ending legs she inherited from him. She is a natural athelete, just as he was. How proud of her he would have been. How I wish they could have known each other.

Our senses and our instincts are failsafe barometers. Sight, smell, sound, taste, and touch serve as witness to our inheritance. They hold us accountable for what has been, these silent tributes that honor a life and keep a bond alive. And so we are compelled to recall, until, after a time, these memories form an interior altar, a place of connection to the dead. Remembering is an act of resurrection, each repetition a vital layer of mourning, in memory of those we are sure to meet again.

Life is serious all the time, but living cannot be. . . .You may have all the solemnity you wish in your neckties, but in anything important—such as sex, death, and religion—you must have mirth or you will have madness.

—G. K. CHESTERTON

FIVE

Death-Defying Humor

My mother told me many times during the course of her life that she was not afraid to die. "Death," she said, "is like opening a door to another adventure."

After she died, I found the following passage tucked away among her papers. It was written a century ago by Henry Scott Holland, a professor of divinity at Oxford University.

> Death is nothing at all—I have only slipped away into the next room. I am I, and you are you. Whatever we were to each other, that we still are. Call me by my old familiar name, speak to me in the easy way you always used. Wear no forced air of solemnity or sorrow. Laugh at the little jokes we enjoyed together. Play, smile, think of me, pray for me. Let my name be ever the household word that it always was. Let it be spoken without the ghost of a shadow on it. Life means all that it ever meant . . . there is absolutely unbroken continuity. I am waiting for you—somewhere near just around the corner.
>
> All is well.

In the same envelope, along with a few photos and post-cards, was a dog-eared cartoon by Roz Chast, clipped from the *New Yorker*. It featured a family—two parents, one dopey-looking kid, a cat, and a dog—all stuck together on their sofa which, in turn, was stuck to the wall along with a couple of lamps and an end table. The caption read: "The Velcros at Home."

To me, this envelope was a treasure trove. The combination of Chast's humor and Holland's prose at once summed up my mother's reverence for the silly and the sublime. Here she was, preserved in a sort of time capsule, before she was taken over by dementia. With this unearthing I had reclaimed her. My mother, who was a sucker for a sight gag and who adored all things English, particularly their trademark turns of phrase. In her first six months in the assisted-living residence (finishing school, she once called it), people assumed she was a visitor rather than an inmate (her word, not mine). Still quite beautiful, with the carriage and theatricality of the fashion model she had once been, my mother would glide into the dining room—tailored suit, alligator handbag, upswept silver chignon, understated jewelry—and as long as she didn't open her mouth, they thought she owned the place.

After a person dies, their personal effects—the flotsam and jetsam collected over a lifetime—become all-important to their survivors. I still wear my mother's engagement ring, and, on occasion, the rose gold Art Deco bracelet my father gave her on their first anniversary, the engraved underside of its links enjoining them still. "To Helen from Ted," it reads. "November 10th, with all my love."

For a long time I couldn't part with a white oxford cloth shirt of my father's, his geometric EAC monogram emblazoned on the breast pocket, or a small green hairbrush threaded with a few strands of my mother's silver hair. The letters they had written to me over the years—his sweet and straightforward, hers punctuated with goofy drawings or off-the-cuff verse— now form a partial biography, living proof of their mark on the world and on me. I once inscribed a book, "To my parents, Helen and Ted Cobb, who couldn't live with or without each other," something my mother said more than once during their thirty-eight-year marriage. They were crazy about each other, but they fought all the time. Humor, the intermittent arbiter, the battle diffuser, was our family's salvation. Without it, their marriage would not have survived.

Dominant personality traits are often the only remnants of dementia. Bullies become more aggressive, introverts withdraw. In my mother's case, humor was operative long after her other hues had faded. In an earlier stage of her Alzheimer's, for instance, soon after she met Maggie, her neighbor on the assisted-living wing who suffered from the same affliction, my mother told me they sat under the gazebo by the lake and told each other "the stories of our lives, and then, fifteen minutes later, forgot everything we said." She told me this in front of Maggie, and as the two of us doubled up in laughter, Maggie, who was actually in better "mental" shape than my mother, sat stone-faced. As I later found out, Maggie had been grumpy for most of her life.

Whatever the extent of the infirmity, I believe the essence of a person—what Carl Jung referred to as the mysterious energy "that lives and endures beneath the eternal flux"—will persevere. This was confirmed many times over in the last week of my mother's life.

The day after she was admitted to hospice, I arrived to find her in the common area, asleep in a kind of chaise longue on wheels, a fire crackling on one side and a television blaring on the other. For some reason the volume was turned up full tilt. (The man in the chair next to hers was very old and probably quite deaf; nonetheless he was riveted to the screen.) The tight ends and linebackers crashing together on the screen took me back to every winter Saturday of my childhood: my father in his enormous leather chair, lost in his football game, the announcer's play-by-play drone infecting the weekend solitude, my mother attempting to read her book in spite of the wall-to-wall din.

She'd say, "It doesn't matter who's playing, your father could watch St. Eucalyptus Prep play the Nativity of the

Blessed Virgin, as long as it's football"—which wasn't entirely true, but it was close. A former Cornell basketball and football player who went on to play semipro football for Syracuse, my father was a lifelong sports devotee who would bellow at anyone who got between him and his game.

"An Ivy League Ralph Kramden, that's you," my mother would say with a mock scowl. My father would laugh and slap his knee, but he would never lower the volume.

And so, when my mother woke up late that Saturday morning, looked at the TV, rolled her eyes, and said, "This is stupid," it was no surprise. The only surprise was that she was able to express it so clearly. In fact, it was only on emerging from a deep sleep that she could form the occasional coherent sentence. Toward the end, her most lucid observations seemed to come sliding out of a dream, an extension of her unconscious, a momentary bridge between the here and her there. The connective tissue, as always, was humor.

"My thoughts exactly, Mom. Hey . . . maybe it's Dad, trying to make contact."

She gave me a little smile, and though I'm not sure she fully understood what I had said, there seemed to be a tiny glimmer of that thing that glued their life together and helped me go on with mine.

When experience is viewed in a certain way,
it presents nothing but doorways into the
domain of the soul, and they are all formed
in the present moment.

—JON KABAT-ZIN

SIX

Telling the Truth

My mother was admitted to hospice on a Friday afternoon in November during a thunderstorm of biblical proportions on the very day I also needed to attend my friend's memorial service, which was to be celebrated behind her house and studio on the land that she loved.

Elaine was fifty-three years old, but unlike my mother, she was not ready to die. I chose to say my final goodbye to her before tending to my mother, a decision I believe each of them would have approved.

The night of Elaine's death I had gone out on our back deck under a full moon—the silence, the shadows of white pine on the moonlit lake, and the chill in the air assured me that Elaine, pantheist to the core, just might be around. Assuming she had already gone straight into active heavenly duty—using even half the dervish-whirling energy that propelled her around the earth—I asked her to help my mother. I'm positive she heard me. My mother was admitted to hospice exactly two weeks later, on that rainy afternoon in November.

I thought of this, standing in the on-and-off downpour

that soaked the overflow of mourners. Despite the weather, clusters of friends and family huddled under and around a large scalloped canopy—some in slickers, some holding umbrellas, all waiting to place their candle at the foot of an altar designed by Elaine's architect husband and built by her youngest son, Mark. As our line moved along, I was amazed that though many of the candles sputtered and hissed, most of them continued to burn. Soon two concentric loops of flame encircled the firepit which lay on the ground before a twelve-foot birch cross, lashed together with strips of leather and backed by three muslin panels that flapped in defiance against the gunmetal sky.

This cathedral, more sacred than most, was made to order for Elaine, whose passion for relics and rituals reached out and galvanized the crowd from beyond the grave.

I picture her two years before her death on a day with identical weather in a hospital corridor in Hartford. Years of living in Mexico City had left Elaine, who was a gorgeous mix of Grace Kelly and Frida Kahlo, with a stable of scarves, skirts, and amulets. She was an exuberant collage embodied in fine-boned bohemian beauty. Adorned in beaded jackets and cowboy boots, or jeans with crimson shawls, she was capable of captivating anyone, anywhere, including a roomful of dispirited cancer patients. Her optimism was infectious and never more so than on that day, when she came bounding down the hall of the radiology wing, eyes shining, necklaces a-clatter, shouting a resounding "*Yes!*" and yielding an upraised fist—the only proclamation we needed to understand that *this* bone scan was cancer-free.

A year later Elaine and her twin sister, Carol, were honored with a twenty-five-year museum retrospective of their work. Their forms of expression were markedly different. While Carol's paintings were figurative, moody dreamscapes— a bed, a barn, a floating pear—Elaine's overlapping layers of textured papers and bold colors were edgy and abstract. Her final canvases, executed at a furious pace during the "up" periods of her last eighteen months, were what she called earth altars or sacred landscapes—pieces of tattered flags, paragraph fragments from yellowed letters penned in the crabbed hand of a great-aunt, string, vintage stamps, pages of old books—that took on an otherworldly quality when banded with a strip of metal, incorporated into a painted skyscape and finally sealed in an encaustic of golden beeswax. As if preserved in amber, the bits and pieces evocative of Elaine's often chaotic world seemed to come together in these last works, a painterly scrapbook of one artist's life.

The twins and their younger brother, Jack, had been born into an artistic family, their teenage lives marked by the death of their mother, of myasthenia gravis, and their father, of alcoholism a decade later. An unspoken and lifelong melancholy surfaced in Carol's and Elaine's works, their disparate styles perhaps reflecting a common grief.

As is the case with most children, neither of them had fully come to terms with the early deaths of their parents. Both girls were at boarding school when their mother died, and Carol cared for their father when he was dying in New York a decade later. Elaine, who was living in Providence at the time, could not bear to witness his last weeks of life and, according to friends, visited only once. Unable to deal with her grief, she retreated completely, a behavior that was to be repeated during her own illness.

During the eight years in which Elaine battled metastatic breast cancer, various friends accompanied her to appointments with oncologists, shamans, surgeons, and radiologists. As the cancer spread, a core group began to evolve, eventually becoming what Elaine called her "healing force."

There were old friends and new friends, most of us freelance artists who lived close to Elaine and had the flexibility to pitch in midday, midweek, as part of a patched-together community. We alternated the responsibilities of driving, cooking, bathing, helping with correspondence, shopping, tidying, massaging—whatever Elaine needed—until our individual efforts stitched together a kind of maternal quilt. We would catch up with one another between "shift changes"—talk, laugh, admire a haircut or new sweater and, out of Elaine's sight line, hold each other and weep. Without even realizing it, we were creating a place of comfort and routine, not only for

Elaine, but for ourselves. Brought together by Elaine's formidable energy and our own desires to help a dear friend, we were now joined by a common need. In retrospect, I realize that many of us were isolated by the nature of our work and longed for this face-to-face connection, a purpose larger than our professional preoccupations.

As Elaine's cancer spread from her bones to the base of her skull and finally to her liver, her pain became unbearable. She was no longer able to paint in her studio, the energy for work, so inextricably entwined with her life force, ebbing daily.

One of the toughest parts of this transitional period was Elaine's inability to acknowledge her growing fear of death. She constantly talked about the cancer, but more as an abstraction than as a life-threatening reality. Avoidance is hard work. Elaine's waning energy was consumed by frantic, circumlocutory monologues—any subject to stonewall the terror. Tiptoeing around the truth must have been especially confusing to her children and her stepchildren, given Elaine's physical appearance. Though the feelings filled the room, they stayed below the surface. The force that had carried Elaine through each grueling metastasis was now used to buffer her denial. We sidestepped the obvious, ill at ease and unable to say what was on all of our minds.

Two months before she died, Elaine told me that the number eighty-four kept cropping up, reinforcing her belief that she would live to see her grandchildren. She was sure, she said, that she would become an old woman. I didn't know what to say. Her fear of death was as fierce as her determination not to speak of it. It was clear that time was short, yet, in moments that begged for communication, family and friends were caught in a conspiratorial web, each paralyzed by uncertainty, unsure how to begin a dialogue and afraid to tread on fragile ground. How could we respect Elaine's fears and remain true to ourselves and the friendship? How could we help her children? How could each of us begin to say goodbye and let Elaine know what she had meant to us?

Only after I read Sherwin Nuland's description of his Aunt Rose in *How We Die* did I decide to reach out to Elaine. His straightforward advice is still the most helpful I have read and I include it here in the hope that it will be for you as well. He writes:

> Without perhaps even realizing it, we had committed one of the worst errors that can be made during a terminal illness—all of us—Rose included, had decided incorrectly and in opposition to every principle of our lives together that it is more important to protect one another from the open admission of a painful truth than it is to achieve a final sharing that might have snatched an enduring comfort and even some dignity from the anguishing fact of death. We denied ourselves what should have been ours.

Although there was no doubt Rose knew she was dying of cancer, we never spoke of it to her, nor did she bring it up. We knew the outlook and so did she; we convinced ourselves she didn't know and we didn't know, though we sensed that she did. So it was like the old scenario that so often throws a shadow over the last days of people with cancer: We Knew, She Knew, We Knew She Knew, She Knew We Knew— and none of us would talk about it when we were together. We kept up the charade to the end. Aunt Rose was deprived, and so were we, of the coming together that should have been, when we might finally tell her what her life had given us. In this sense, my Aunt Rose died alone.

This passage—and this passage alone—gave me the courage to risk putting on paper what I had been unable to say. Following are exerpts from that letter I wrote to Elaine six weeks before her death:

    . . . I have longed to talk to you on a deeper level, like we did on the ferry ride to the Vineyard. [A small group of us had gone to Martha's Vineyard to celebrate her birthday the previous June.] Yet I fear— because the cancer is in your liver and because I am going away for a month—we may never have this conversation, even though its roots are in my heart . . . I have been amazed by your tenacity, by your fierce will to live, moved by the emotion you express through your work . . . but face-to-face I sometimes feel at a great distance from you, as if I am on the shore watching you tread water with increasing effort and strain. If in reality I were there, surely I would throw you a lifeline. And so, symbolically, I throw it now. Your stepchildren and your children are waiting. I think we all are. What should we do? How shall we be? How can we comfort you? Perhaps we, more than you, need that lifeline . . .

Encouraging communication and respecting the rights of the dying require a delicate balance, yet there comes a time when it is crucial not to hold back what is in our hearts. When the dying have departed, we have no reprieves, no time to say what might have been said, to write what might have been written. It is the living, after all, who are left to grieve. If this grief is complicated by regret, the psychic burden is heavier still.

It was scary to send that letter, but I felt it was unnatural to remain silent. I did not hear from Elaine for the month I was away—something I had feared and half-expected—and when she told a mutual friend about the letter, all she could say was, "The cancer is in my liver, that doesn't mean I'm . . ." but she didn't finish the sentence.

When I returned, I visited Elaine. She was extremely weak. A full-time home hospice worker was now on duty. As we sat in silence on her back porch, rays of light filtered through the ornamental grasses she had planted the previous summer. I read poetry—she especially liked Mary Oliver—rubbed her feet, brushed her hair. We held hands. She closed her eyes and soaked in the last of the afternoon sun. After a long silence, she pushed herself up with considerable effort and asked, "How is your mother?"

"Well, I . . . she . . . I really think she's trying to die, Elaine."

Elaine nodded and said simply, "Yes. I know."

Elaine's daughter Tessa later told me that a week later, sitting in the very same spot, when she could "no longer hold it together," she collapsed in sobs at her mother's side. And once again, Elaine said, in acknowledgment, "I know, Tessa, I know."

When Tessa and I compared our experiences, we both felt that Elaine's simple statement signaled a shift in attitude, an acceptance.

On that autumn afternoon, for the first time in a long time, my beautiful friend, although unbelievably thin and pale, was serene. When I leaned down to kiss her goodbye, she awakened and grabbed my hand.

"Thank you for being my friend," she whispered, tears flooding her eyes.

I say now as I said then, "Thank you, Elaine, for being mine; how much I learned from you."

In the following days, the home hospice team began to prepare the family for what to expect—physically, emotionally, and spiritually—and how to ease Elaine's transition from this world to the next. At this crucial juncture one person's distress, even if unconsciously manifested, can effect the dynamic of an entire group. Terminal illness seems to bring out the best and the worst in families. I have heard more than one story about people "retreating" into automatic behaviors only later to be plagued by their own carelessness.

In one family, a known but outwardly unacknowledged alcoholic set up a bar on the far side of the living room where her brother lay dying, and insisted on serving drinks to everyone who visited. This created an awkward situation, but no one wanted to confront a long-standing problem at such a sacrosanct time. Finally the home hospice nurse took a few family members aside and told them in no uncertain terms that "the angels would never come with all the booze around."

Her admonition gave the family the permission they needed. The bar was disassembled, a caveat was issued, and a more open consensus prevailed, one that probably saved them years of familial resentment.

We all need the gentle encouragement to be more "present" around a deathbed. According to hospice literature, as a person is dying, two entities are at work: the body and the spirit. As the body begins to shut down, a progressive series of changes—in heart rate, breathing, kidney function—take place until finally the organs stop functioning altogether. At the same time, the spirit is beginning to separate from the body and from its earthbound ties. If there is unfinished business, an issue or a relationship that remains unsettled, the person is prone to linger until a resolution takes place. Sometimes the spirit may be resolved before the body is ready to go.

Often the dying see things that we do not. It is important to honor these visions. My mother saw "faces" around her bed and then told me she was "so happy." A few days before Elaine died, she reached out and said, "I'm coming, Mother, I'm coming." Although I have heard stories like these again and again, many people remain skeptical. For those who have trouble believing, ask a friend or a neighbor, a minister or rabbi. One of them is bound to have a story or two that reinforces my belief in the many I have heard. For those who need firsthand experience, be patient. Your time will come.

A gradual catharsis came in the last week of Elaine's life. With respect to her family's privacy, it is important to know that *what* was said is less important than the fact that it *was* said. This was a time of renewal, a true coming together, an opportunity to review, to forgive, to celebrate Elaine's life, and to openly mourn her passing.

Even at the time of death new rituals may be born. As the women in Elaine's family bathed her, dressed her, smoothed lotion on her frail limbs, and combed her still-luxuriant hair, the men in her family constructed a cairn in a clearing near the house. This conical monument of stones from the surrounding fields was an earth altar constructed in homage to Elaine. After three days of dawn-to-dusk labor, the men finished the job which, her son later told me, felt "meditative and, in a strange way, celebrative." The entire family believed that Elaine, who died hours later, just before midnight, had waited for its completion.

Preparing for a death by creating meaningful rituals encourages emotional catharsis and spiritual release. And acknowledging family dynamics, in spite of the helpless and painful feelings, helps us move toward a resolution, however imperfect it may be.

We are fortunate when we have the time—the luxury, really—to say goodbye, particularly if it's under the guidance of hospice workers. These are the people who teach us that the end of life requires an awareness that transcends the confines of traditional medicine. The work that was started half a century ago by Dame Cicely Saunders—director of St. Christopher's Hospice in England and founder, along with Elisabeth Kübler-Ross, of the modern hospice movement—continues all over the world today. No matter what our religious beliefs, we share a common humanity. Palliative care is based on this principle, in the tending to the physical and emotional needs of the dying, in the recognition of the mystery of life's final cycle, and in the realization that there is a time to hold on and a time to let go. Coming to terms with these very basic tenets will better prepare us for the two roles that we must each adopt over the course of our lives—as the living with the dying and as the dying with the living. Though our scripts will differ, our need to understand them will not.

Death forces a grace period on all of us. The dying offer the living a final chance to be the best that they can be. We must take our cues from them, value the moments that lead up to and follow their departure, and work toward acceptance after they are gone. This is a vow as sacred as any we will make over the course of our lifetimes.

The Dead

The dead are always looking down on us, they say,
while we are putting on our shoes or making a sandwich,
they are looking down through the glass-bottom boats of heaven
as they row themselves slowly through eternity.

They watch the tops of our heads moving below on earth,
and when we lie down in a field or on a couch,
drugged perhaps by the hum of a warm afternoon,
they think we are looking back at them,

which makes them lift their oars and fall silent
and wait, like parents, for us to close our eyes.

—BILLY COLLINS

SEVEN

Dreaming

In the days following a death, survivors become acutely attuned to the subtext of human behavior, developing a kind of laser vision and a newfound courage, which in some situations may lead to empathy, in others to impatience. Reentry into the world can be a jarring experience for those in mourning, and a short fuse is often the offshoot of prolonged suffering.

Shortly after my mother died, I attended a dinner party where a well-known television correspondent who had just returned from assignment in Paris was to be the guest of honor. When the newsman arrived, well past the point of de rigueur, he swaggered through the front door—one massive retriever in tow, one wife bringing up the rear—clad in grey flannels, navy blazer, pink shirt, and paisley pocket scarf, in a cloud of his own Gauloises smoke. He was short, with a large head.

As the evening progressed, he pontificated and postured, smoked between courses, snarled at his spouse and sweet-talked his canine, his slavering more lavish with each glass of bordeaux. This excessive attention proved tacit encouragement for his pooch—equipped with a bread-box-sized head, a table-clearing tail, and horrific halitosis—to probe each guest's nap-kined lap as his master held court.

Like all tyrants—the loudmouth on the cell phone in your train car or the popcorn chomper who narrates each movie scene before it transpires—this fellow's self-absorption bordered on assault.

Would you have the temerity to bring your dog to a dinner party, let alone ignore his table manners? Would you tolerate someone smoking up the dining room and monopolizing the conversation? Would you muzzle your own insubordination in order to accommodate his?

Although avoiding confrontation encourages this kind of behavior, most of us continue to err on the side of politesse. Whether it's tyranny by entitlement, as in this fellow's case, or simply tyranny by stupidity, we tolerate the intolerable far too often.

Except, curiously, during times of crisis, when circumstances force us to adopt a take-no-prisoners policy. When our emotional reserves are limited, we know instinctively what we will and will not abide and where and when to draw the line.

Although my truest response was stifled by propriety, I found a way to work out my frustration. When we stumble during our waking hours, the unconscious walks us through alternative solutions. These nocturnal revisions, at least for me, provide a certain satisfaction, a dream-induced retrospective spleen-venting—what I call REM Revenge.

My postdinner party dream was set in a narrow, multisto-ried, lopsided Victorian house askew in a fractured-fairy-tale kind of way. A raucous party was in progress on every floor. Guests were wedged together, cheek by jowl, standing in stair-wells, crouched under the piano, draped over banisters, clutch-ing drinks, air-kissing and cackling, all over the din of Muzak and high-pitched nonstop conversation. Their gestures and laughter were wildly exaggerated. No one listened. Everyone talked. The scene was surreal and claustrophobic—Buñuel à la Brueghel—and I was desperate to get out. After trying several dead-end doors, I found one which led to an outdoor deck that backed up to a craggy, vertical peak many times higher than the house. The silence and the cold night air were a soothing con-trast to the cacophony inside; the moonlit sky and the snow-capped mountain seemed to beckon. In an instant I decided to shoot, as it were, for the stars. With a bow to the combined spirits of Peter Pan and Norman Vincent Peale, thinking lovely and positive thoughts, I achieved liftoff, flying up over the mountain and into the night, the house now a tiny speck on the ground below.

Would that it were so easy to leave our troubles behind. The intermittent flying dreams I have had since childhood helped me escape a whole slew of bad scenes. I awake refreshed, each dream a momentary, if illusory, reprieve.

My last fantasy flight occurred two years ago, on the night my mother died—a most astonishing dream, markedly differ-ent from any of my previous flying dreams, more symbolic of elation than escape. For starters, it was a sunny day. I was wearing a voluminous fuchsia cape, which billowed behind me as I soared and swooped and sang an improvisational aria in my best coloratura soprano—or at least that's how it seemed in the dream. My voice was passionate and fully realized, almost as if this were the performance of a lifetime. I cruised over undulating meadows and vast pockets of Technicolor wildflowers; children frolicked and tumbled with abandon as bees and butterflies buzzed and fluttered in storybook profusion. My aerial view was lush and panoramic, as if I could indefinitely sustain this connection to the people below who smiled and applauded and waved me on my way. This was a dramatic departure from all my previous nocturnal takeoffs, which had been solo, furtive, with nary a witness in sight. I was unafraid—soaring on pure delight.

An equally powerful dream followed the next night. Picture a freeze-frame of a single image: a flickering candle whose base is formed by interlocking pieces of wood that have been smoothed and crafted into a glossy dome. That's all it was. One candle. No people. No movement or light, except for the candle's flame. Try as I might to change the image while I was dreaming, I could not, though I can remember thinking in my dream, Is this a dream?

I have since come to the conclusion that the candle's intractability signaled permanence; its flame, hope; its dovetailed base—a series of complex, hard-to-fit, tightly assembled elements—integration; and its female shape and undimmed light, a metaphor for rebirth.

In Dreamspeak, flying symbolizes "transcendent awareness" and a candle represents "that which ignites our spiritual talents and abilities." With the help of my unconscious, the darkness I had lived with during the years of my mother's and Elaine's illnesses had been lifted. I was filled with a sense of hope.

Most of us experience a kind of hyperconsciousness before and after the death of someone we love. When we "pool" the individual dreams that grow out of a shared situation, we create a collective reel of images, each frame adding a new dimension to the overall picture.

The night before my mother died, my husband dreamt that the two of them were driving along a curvy mountain road with a thicket of greenery on one side and a steep drop-off on the other. She was sitting quite close to him—there was no center console in his dream car—and wore what he describes as a beautiful lilac-colored dress, cloudlike, swirling around her. My mother was smiling and pointing in front of her, giving my husband directions, showing him the way. When he recounted the dream to me and I asked him how he felt about it, he said he was not only amazed by the vivid images but by the clarity of his communication with my mother—for the last year of her life we had to hold up both ends of the conversation with her—and said that he felt my mother was finally at peace.

An invisible cord tethers me to the people I have loved who have died. They are there as long as I am here; we are joined in our absence and our presence, our future and our past. Dreams may be the clearest conduit to the eternal continuum. The dead speak through us. Our job is to listen and recall, to instill in our children the significance of the humility and the humanity that every loss evokes, and to let them know that their character will be shaped by who they are, not by what they do.

Perhaps it is only when we realize and celebrate the intrinsic value of every human life that celebrity—true celebrity—shines most brightly. On our deathbeds, none of us will speak of the jobs we've held or the stuff we've acquired in our lifetimes; here bull markets and Nielsen ratings are irrelevant. A life-threatening illness jettisons pretension in no time flat. Death is the great equalizer. Death dares us to define what really matters.

Mortals and immortals,
Living in each others' death,
Dying in each others' life.

—HERACLITUS

Eight

The Saints and the Poets

Over the past six years I have interviewed a cross section of people—mostly writers and poets. I like to think of this period as my late-bloomer graduate work, a broad-brush tutorial in what makes us tick, and an extended course in learning to listen.

As the host of a public radio program, I was thrilled that my first interview was to be with Annie Dillard, since two of her books, *Pilgrim at Tinker Creek* and *An American Childhood,* are among my favorites.

On a steamy July afternoon, as soon as her neighbor's lawnmower had been retired, the producer, the sound man, and I squeezed into a small writing shed in Dillard's backyard in Middletown, Connecticut, set up our equipment, and began to record her reluctant musings. Her delivery, characterized by a voice made gravelly from years of smoking and late-night pinochle, was not at all what I expected; if truth be told, I thought she would fall somewhere between Walden Pond and Joni Mitchell. Annie Dillard was a surprise but certainly not a disappointment. I liked her lack of sentimentality, her scrappy approach to just about everything. But what I liked best was her inability to take herself too seriously.

At age twenty-seven, Dillard learned she had won the Pulitzer prize when an AP reporter called her one evening as she was preparing dinner.

"Is this Annie Dillard?" he yelled into the receiver.

"Yes, it is."

"What are you doing this very minute?"

"Uh . . . I'm washing spinach," Dillard said.

"Well," he bellowed, "you'll never have to wash spinach again! You've just won the Pulitzer prize!"

Recalling the moment, Dillard, deadpan, shrugged her shoulders as if to say, What a concept.

Humility is as much a guarantor of self-awareness as hubris is its detractor. Annie Dillard and writers of her ilk are truth tellers, prone to give voice to their "own astonishment," as Dillard wrote in an essay for the *New York Times Book Review* a decade ago.

"Write as if you were dying," she said. "At the same time, write for an audience consisting solely of terminal patients. That is, after all, the case."

Perspective of this magnitude does not come easily, of course, particularly if you are a writer with even a scintilla of insecurity, writing a book about *death,* no less. A few years ago (or perhaps weeks) a statement like this would have sent me packing. I'd have closed down this computer for good and gone underground.

The kind of rigorous standard that Dillard espouses requires a creative ruthlessness, a daily monitoring of psyche and soul, a cognizance of one's own short run on the planet. But indeed the world would be a kinder place if we could apply Dillard's writing advice to our lives, like a poultice to a wounded spirit. How many more times, after all, will we watch a harvest moon ease over the horizon and erupt into a full-blown gold or catch a winter sunrise as it turns a field of snow to sparkling? Only when we name these wonders do we realize how evanescent their brightness, how finite their encores.

Emerson once suggested that if there were but one starlit night a year everyone on the planet would stop to herald the annual pageant of light. An amended version of Emerson's idyll happens on alternate Wednesday evenings from mid-June through late August in Farmington, Connecticut, where the Sunken Garden Poetry Festival has grown and flourished. What began as a brainstorm between two journalists and one teacher-poet has since become a destination for the fledgling and the veteran poetry lover alike. Imagine. Poetry, not cramped behind a dais in some dusty lecture hall, but alight on summer breezes amid lush foliage. It's a kind of fantastic reality for everyone: poets, radio crew, museum personnel, corporate sponsors, families, friends, grandparents, groundskeepers, and kids with multiple piercings who gather on blankets and lawn chairs around a central latticed gazebo flanked by brick pathways and tulip trees. Musicians—the "warm-up acts"—have ranged from flutist Rhonda Larson to the the steel drum ensemble Pan Caribé.

Mapped out at the turn of the century by landscape architect Beatrix Farrand, this walled sanctuary of hedgerows and perennials is the jewel in the crown of 150 acres now known as the Hill-Stead Museum. Once the home of industrialist and art collector Alfred Pope, this Colonial Revival "country house" designed by his daughter, Theodate, today accommodates an extraordinary collection of French and American Impressionists. Paintings by Degas, Manet, and Whistler; Cassatt's babies and Monet's haystacks comfortably share space with mahogany highboys, tufted settees, and worn Persian carpets in an environment so intimate one can easily imagine the Popes on their veranda after a leisurely game of croquet, sipping iced tea, quoting Coleridge, Keats, or even that renegade, Blake.

Many festival fans believe that the Popes have given their posthumous blessing to the sound of poetry on these heavenly grounds. And why not? Poetry speaks to the souls of the living as it gives voice to the dead. Richard Wilbur, Sue Ellen Thompson, Stanley Kunitz, Carolyn Forché, Billy Collins, Eamon Grennan, Kate Rushin, Galway Kinnell, Mark Doty, Margaret Gibson, Hayden Carruth, and Lucille Clifton were just some of the poets whose verses entwined past and present, each poet an archivist, a witness, an explorer; each poem a memory, an elegy, a psalm. In fact, out of the more than thirty visiting poets so far, there have been only two oddballs in an otherwise engaging bunch—one who exuded a kind of Imelda Marcos hauteur and another whose affect can only be described as faux Bo Peep. Even with poets, the bell curve applies.

Donald Hall's first reading many months after the death of his forty-seven-year-old wife, the poet Jane Kenyon, took place in the Sunken Garden. The evening was a collaboration of his work and hers, many of the poems coming from her collection *Otherwise,* published the year after she died. Kenyon selected the cover art for that volume just after they had composed her obituary days before her death—Gustave Caillebotte's *Le Jardin Potager, Yerres.* It features a walled garden crisscrossed by rose-colored pathways and strips of muted light and shadow. A passionate gardener, Kenyon wrote of the commonplace with what Hayden Carruth called "a rare and somber grace." A small stone, a clothespin, an old flannel nightgown, a blue bowl, an apron, a peony at dusk—Kenyon's spare poems illuminate the ordinary with a rare brand of alchemy that makes us catch our breath.

I met Jane Kenyon once, when she came to a writer's workshop in New Haven taught by a mutual friend. There were seven members in our Monday night group, half of us trying our hand at poetry, the other half at fiction. I struggled with the poetic form, given my penchant for rambling, and tried hard to fit my run-on narratives into dignified stanzas.

The night Jane sat in, I read the third draft of a poem about my father's suicide and after class told Jane how much I had admired her poems that tackled her bouts with the blues. "Having It Out with Melancholy" puts flesh on the bones of despair like nothing I have ever read. The poem is a startlingly visceral and eloquent description of her lifelong battle with depression.

Little did I know that three years after meeting Jane Kenyon, I would be laid low by my own depression, a depression professionals call "situational" rather than "chronic," a depression that oozed out of a confluence of events: Elaine's cancer, my mother's newly diagnosed Alzheimer's disease, echoes of my father's death and—how can I say this graciously—a surfeit of narcissists in my life.

The inability to sleep, to eat, to walk the dog, to form a coherent sentence, to read a paragraph, is a terrifying experience. It seemed as though my spirit was entombed for good. But, bit by bit, with the help of some amazing friends I gradually, and I mean gradually, emerged from my zombie state. Today, I refer to this period as my Reptile Phase and can still remember well the feeling of hauling my clammy, scaly, low-to-the-ground self through each interminable day—and night.

Coming out of a depression, I suppose, is a bit like coming back from the dead. It's learning to breathe again. And it is certainly as humbling to rediscover the most basic of life's pleasures as it is to lose them.

Thornton Wilder won a Pulitzer prize for a play that he said was his "attempt to find a value above all price for the smallest events in our daily life." Sixty years later, *Our Town* is still being performed all over the world. Go see it if you have a chance. Even a high school production will break your heart.

The play's denouement comes near the end of the third act and features Emily, who has died at the age of twenty-seven in childbirth, returning from the world of the dead to the living for one last look at her life in Grover's Corners. She chooses the morning of her twelfth birthday, and as she watches the day unfold, she is staggered by the simple gifts of the life she once had on earth—"the ticking clocks and Mama's sunflowers, the food, the coffee, the new ironed dresses and the hot baths, the sleeping and the waking up." As an observer of the world she once inhabited, Emily is acutely aware of what she has left behind. She bursts into tears and asks the play's narrator, "Do any humans ever realize life while they live it? Every, every minute?"

He pauses for a minute. "No," he says, shaking his head sadly, and then, after some reflection, allows for the following: "The saints and the poets, maybe—they do some."

Wilder's words reverberate in a poem by Jane Kenyon, composed soon after her husband's second cancer operation. Twenty years Kenyon's senior, Donald Hall said they always assumed, even before his cancer, that because of his age, he would be the "first to go." However, some months after Hall's cancer went into remission, Jane Kenyon was diagnosed with leukemia and, after fifteen hard-won months, died in the bedroom of their New Hampshire home, Eagle Pond Farm.

OTHERWISE

I got out of bed
on two strong legs.
It might have been
otherwise. I ate
cereal, sweet
milk, ripe flawless
peach. It might
have been otherwise.
I took the dog uphill
to the birch wood.
All morning I did
the work I love.

At noon I lay down
with my mate. It might
have been otherwise.
We ate dinner together
at a table with silver

candlesticks. It might
have been otherwise.
I slept in a bed
in a room with paintings
on the walls, and
planned another day
just like this day.
But one day, I know,
it will be otherwise.

—JANE KENYON

We help each other——even unconsciously, each in our own effort, we lighten the effort of others——sorrow comes in great waves . . . but it rolls over us, and though it may almost smother us it leaves us on the spot and we know that if it is strong we are stronger, inasmuch as it passes and we remain.

—HENRY JAMES

NINE

Unnatural Losses

Now that I am a mother, I cannot conceive of losing a child to death. Yet every month, it seems, we are confronted with this very reality. Whether it occurs in our schoolyards or our backyards, in a hospital or on a highway, we weep for the children of the world. The horrors we witness leave us bereft—from Paducah, Kentucky, to Oklahoma City, from Northern Ireland to central Scotland, from Kosovo to Brazil, from a side street in Detroit to a fence post in Wyoming to a high school in Colorado.

Sixteen tiny plots in the Dunblane cemetery represent an entire kindergarten class and their teacher slain by a madman. A three-word inscription on one of the gravestones—OUR WEE MAN—speaks volumes of one family's grief and of any parent's whose child predeceases them.

William Sloan Coffin, the outspoken theologian and social reformer, delivered a sermon to his congregation at New York's Riverside Church ten days after the death of his son. Here is the beginning of that spare and tender tribute:

As almost all of you know, a week ago last Monday night, driving in a terrible storm, my son Alexander—who to his friends was a real day brightener, and to his family, "fair as a star when only one is shining in the sky"—my twenty-four-year-old Alexander, who enjoyed beating his old man at every game and in every race, beat his father to the grave.

Among the healing flood of letters that followed his death was one carrying this wonderful quote from the end of Hemingway's *Farewell to Arms.* "The world breaks everyone, then some become strong at the broken places." My own broken heart is mending, largely thanks to so many of you, my dear parishioners; for if in the last week I have relearned one lesson, it is that love not only begets love, it transmits strength.

I learned about the strength of which Coffin speaks from my dear friend Connie, who lives with her family in a small town in Holland, a town where her son died a week after his sixteenth birthday on a cold January day.

Connie has spoken often of her last moments with Christian that morning before he flew out the door, grinning, guitar case in one hand, backpack in the other, a broad-brimmed hat disguising the Walkman she had bought him for Christmas.

She also remembers a warning voice running through her head in the store as she was about to purchase the Walkman. "Don't buy it," the voice said. But Christian, being Christian, had been bugging her about one for months. "Don't buy it." He had to have one, all the other kids had theirs. "Don't buy it." In spite of her misgivings, Connie did.

Christian lived for music. He played in a band and spent much of his free time working on chord arrangements or listening to his tapes. That morning he was en route to Amsterdam to buy tickets for an upcoming concert.

"Sure you don't want to come along, Mom?" he called over his shoulder.

If only she had. Connie says she must live with that regret for the rest of her life. Regrets, as so many people have told me, haunt the living long after tragedies occur. But as Connie says, the "if onlys" could drive one to near madness, and she decided she must "get past them" for the sake of her husband, Christian's brother, her stepchildren, and herself.

That morning in January, Christian spotted the westbound train in the distance, rushed past the flashing red lights, ducked under the black and white crossbar—as the kids always did at this suburban railway stop—and was struck by the high-speed eastbound train he couldn't hear over the blare of his Walkman. But Connie believes there were "signs" before that morning.

As she describes it, there were moments that seemed to signal Christian's foreshortened life. He dreamt of a train accident that he related in detail. He declared, just weeks before his death, that when he died he hoped it would be with his guitar. For much of that year Connie had experienced a persistent feeling of dread. During the days before his death Connie wept "without stop" and frequently went into his room to "kiss Christian as he slept—while I still could." Two weeks before he died, Connie had an overwhelming sensation that a "giant whoosh would sweep Christian away." Connie's premonition was so disturbing she confided it to a friend, in spite of the fact that she was as terrified to voice it as not to.

In the days that followed Christian's death Connie says a strange sense of certainty and resolve, along with a growing faith, began to emerge in her.

"It was a completely intuitive process," she says. "Somehow, in the moment when I realized—when I actually accepted that Christian was dead—I knew what I had to do. It was as if I were being carried by God. This gave me strength. I remembered that Christian had been so peaceful, so inward, the week before he died—almost as if he knew—just as I knew, somehow, that I had to take care of myself for Christian so that his sweet soul could fly free."

How, I wondered, would she, would any of us, begin to comfort another parent who had lost a child.

"I would hold them," she said. "Hold them and rock them and let them know I understand."

I had considered interviewing other friends of friends— families in New York and Washington, in San Francisco and South Carolina—families whose children have also died violently, families who had no precognition of their children's deaths, families whose lives have been equally and irrevocably shattered by such a horrible turn of events. But after talking to Connie I realized that her story is a universal one.

The despair that follows the death of a young person—whether by illness, violence, or sudden accident—is unimaginable. Yet wherever we find strength, I believe, as Connie does, that the power of touch and the ability to embrace and to listen are the most human and universal gifts we can offer and receive. If we have the courage to communicate this love in the face of immeasurable despair, if we can extend ourselves and acknowledge another's sorrow, we will pass along a valuable lesson to future generations.

No matter what our level of understanding, whether child or adult, it is vital to acknowledge our feelings after someone we love dies. Although we should not expect one person or belief system to serve up the perfect sacrament, we should each make an attempt to listen and to respond, to remain open, even though our inclination may be to withdraw completely in the wake of our own anxiety or in the assumption that mourning requires privacy. It may not. Grief needs a place to go, months or even years after a death occurs. With friends, family, neighbors, or acquaintances, at home or in the workplace, it is important to be aware of their loss well beyond the first few weeks of mourning. Let them know you care and, moreover, that you remember. Remaining silent or acting as if everything is "back to normal" will only amplify their sense of isolation.

Many people have told me they "don't know what to say"

to the family of someone who has died and, sadly, for fear of saying the "wrong thing," end up saying nothing at all. People in mourning need our support. In times of sorrow, one word, one gesture, can mean everything.

Each one of us must take the initiative. Hold someone's hand. Send a poem, a photograph, a letter of remembrance. If you buy a condolence card, add a personal message. If you feel awkward, simply say, "I've been thinking of you." This will create an opening. Don't ask what you can do. Anticipate and act. Listen. Be compassionate. Don't give advice, philosophize, or tell the person you know how they're feeling. You don't. Statements such as "It was God's will" or "Your loved one is better off now" are insensitive sentiments, akin to a poke with a sharp stick. It's best to be true to yourself and to the person who has died. If you knew them well, create a picture, a memory of a time you spent together, for his or her family—a night at the movies, an afternoon over a cup of tea, an ongoing joke only known to the two of you—the most common recollection has uncommon meaning for people in mourning, particularly if it's a story they've never heard. You have different memories than they do. Think of your reminiscence as a tiny eulogy, an addition to their family archives, and know that if it comes with compassion the contribution will be welcome.

The president of the public television and radio station where I have worked told me that he and his family have drawn com-

fort from some of the most surprising sources since the acci-
dental death of his thirteen-year-old son last year. Of the many
letters the family received, "the most poignant by far, the one
most filled with love, with humanity" came from an electronics
technician at Jerry's station, a station that has had a history of
adversarial relations between labor and management.

"We have had some tough union battles over the years,"
Jerry says, "that put us squarely on opposite sides of the fence,
and yet, when I saw this man on my first day back at work, I
thanked him for his letter, which had touched me so deeply, and
he put his arms around me and held me without saying a word."

A month later, when Jerry went to his neighborhood gas
station for an oil change, John, the mechanic who has serviced
his cars for a decade, crossed the grease-slicked floor, arms
extended toward Jerry, and kissed him on both cheeks, and as
Jerry says, the two of them "stood there crying, locked in an
embrace, amidst tools and tires and a garage full of men."

Jerry's son, Alexander, was, by anyone's standards, an
unusual boy. At a standing-room-only memorial service in the
gymnasium of a local school whose motto, "Catch the Spirit,"
was painted in bold purple script on the cinderblock wall, students, coaches, teachers, and friends gathered to remember
Alex. They spoke of his ebullience, his moxie, and his remark-
able list of accomplishments.

His music teacher said he was one of those rare "triple hit-
ters," a member of the choir, the band, and the orchestra. His

classmates Julie, Katie, David, and Laura played one of Alex's favorite pieces by Mozart: "Eine Kleine Nachtmusik." His friend David played the cello: "The Swan" by Saint-Saens. Ian, wearing a blue soccer shirt with a red number 9 on the back, played Elton John's "Can You Feel the Love Tonight" on the piano.

Alex, dubbed "the Pit Bull" by his teammates, had traveled with them to Europe the previous summer for an international soccer competition. In recalling Alex's athletic ability and competitive spirit, the coach looked up at the sky and talked to him directly. "There's going to be a big hole in our defense, Alex, as well as in our hearts."

"This year's baseball season will be dedicated to our shortstop, Alex," the coach said, "and every player will wear his number, 4, on their uniform, in addition to their own." The coach's hearing-impaired son, Anthony, signed and read aloud a piece he had written for Alex, particularly touching for the simplicity of its final sentence: "I will miss you."

An honor student as well as a track and basketball star, Alex was on the road to becoming an Eagle Scout. But mostly Alex was remembered by his classmates as a "great guy with a good sense of humor." As his Boy Scout troop (170) led the opening and closing flag and candle ceremonies, Alex, handsome, self-possessed, arms akimbo, peered out at them—at all of us—from a poster-sized photograph on an easel behind a table of memorabilia: a baseball glove, a soccer ball, a cello, a French horn, a sashful of scout badges; this towhead with the bowl haircut, a half smile, and dark eyes that sparkled with a hint of devilry was, one couldn't help thinking, too good to be true, a feeling echoed in the Robert Frost poem read by his elementary school principal, "Nothing Gold Can Stay."

Alex's death changed an entire community overnight. Children, most of whom had never before experienced a death, let alone the death of a peer, worked side by side with parents and teachers to create loving rituals to honor their classmate's life. Because of the care they took in preparing and presenting their final tributes, they will heal more fully and they will remember their friend Alex, as well as their own first encounter with grief, for the rest of their lives.

We all expect to experience a parent's death one day, but never a child's. It is as unnatural as it is unimaginable and resonates here in the final paragraph of William Coffin's eulogy to his son:

> When parents die, as did my mother last month, they take with them a large portion of the past. But when children die, they take away the future as well. That is what makes the valley of the shadow of death seem so incredibly dark and unending. In a prideful way it would be easier to walk the valley alone, nobly, head high, instead of—as we must—marching along as the latest recruit in the world's army of the bereaved.

The medium is the message.

—MARSHALL MCLUHAN

TEN

Hannah Lee

Signing my mother's hospice admittance papers on the morning of Elaine's memorial service, I realized it was the eighth of November. My parents' wedding anniversary was November 10, my father had died on November 15, and my mother, as it turned out, would die on November 17. Exactly twenty years before Elaine's memorial service, to the week, a documentary film called *Hannah Lee,* depicting a day in the life of a dying woman, was completed not far from the town where Elaine had lived. I was amazed by the echoes of events two decades later and have since come to believe that my real work—what Thomas Moore refers to as one's daimon and Joseph Campbell one's bliss—might just be linked to this full, synchronous circle.

Hannah Lee Beck was my friend. Struggling with juvenile diabetes for twenty-seven of her thirty-six years, she had lived and worked in New York City until the complications of the disease—kidney failure that required thrice-weekly dialysis and caused failing eyesight and severe neuropathy, a deadening of the nerve endings that makes walking nearly impossible—forced her to move back to Connecticut with her mother.

Hannah Lee, only a dozen years my senior, was the first person I had known close to my age who lived with a life-threatening illness. We met when I was a student at the American Academy of Dramatic Arts and she was working for *Newsweek,* three years before leaving New York. She came to see me in a play, and afterward, we had coffee.

Hannah Lee was a beautiful woman, tall and slim, with the grace of the athelete she once had been and the gutsy determination that made her begin braille lessons just days after she went blind. When we got together, there was an intensity, even an urgency, to our conversations. There were few subjects we didn't cover in detail, and she spoke with a candor and self-scrutiny that perhaps only a shadowed life allows.

By the time she moved to Connecticut, we had had several heart-to-heart conversations about dying. Though she was afraid of death, she said, she was not afraid to talk about it or about the difficulties that accompanied her disease. What really galled her was the way she and her fellow patients were sometimes patronized by the staff of the dialysis unit. Once, after she went blind, she said she heard a friend of hers moaning and asked one of the nurses if he was in pain. The nurse told Hannah that he was just "asleep and dreaming."

"I knew it wasn't true," she said, "I knew that he was suffering, and I don't want to be lied to like that—none of us do."

Hannah Lee was passionate about getting to the truth and had little time for regret; her rare complaint was reserved for the restrictions of her disease or for the indescretions of her "fast-track life in Paris" during her twenties. Only once, she told me, was she so overwhelmed by what would never be—"the husband, the children, the white picket fence"—that she "couldn't speak for days." Much of the time, though, she was incredibly optimistic, anxious to talk about her latest book or concert on tape and equally curious about what I had read or seen and what jobs I had auditioned for. She wanted, she said, to "stay in touch with the world for as long as was humanly possible."

In spite of her blindness, she kept up her subscription to New Haven's Long Wharf Theater and it was there that we attended Michael Christofer's *Shadow Box*, a Pulitzer prize–winning play set in a hospice, about four different families coping with terminal illness. Describing the sets, the costumes, the actors' faces, and watching her own as she strained to hear every word of the dialogue that she could well have written made the drama doubly poignant for both of us.

After the theater, on the train ride back to New York where I had an early audition the next morning, I thought about the day. About Hannah Lee. About how much I would have liked to play a character in *Shadow Box* or *Hedda Gabler* instead of the housewife I had played in a Drano commercial the week before. Costumed in ill-fitting khakis, a polyester shirt, and white Keds—not unlike the several housewife ensembles always audition-ready in the back of my closet—I had tried my best to express moral outrage over the state of my drain, as if my very life depended on its free-flowing efficiency.

Although the first line—"My sink trap's clogged with grease"—dripped with Chekovian dolor, I couldn't make it work. Actually, I wasn't quite sure what a sink trap was.

In addition to unclogging drains, I vacuumed rugs, fluffed laundry, drank coffee, dusted living rooms, guzzled soft drinks, poured cereal, and middle-managed. In other words, I gave feminism a bad name. My reward for playing moms, mortgage brokers, and housewives was two Union cards—SAG (Screen Actors Guild) and AFTRA (American Federation of Television and Radio Artists)—decent health benefits, and, for an added bonus, a backlog of character-building rejection. If you've ever worried that you're not thin enough, young enough, short enough, cute enough, or ethnic enough, become an actor. It will be confirmed.

I stuck it out for two years, until Stanislavsky's advice to the stage actor morphed into an ever-deafening mantra: Where have I come from? What do I want? Where am I going?

Hannah Lee relished my growing cynicism. At her urging I gladly held forth on the characters I encountered each week: a director who took half the day to perfect the juxtaposition of milk carton and cereal box, a producer who cautioned us to "stop fractionating and focus," a gum-snapping receptionist clad from head to toe in silver lamé, an *All About Eve* competitor, and a power-crazed acting coach, who, after years of Janovian primal scream therapy had begun to confuse the art of scene study with headshrinking. In order to "come from a more open place" in our prepared monologues, this thespian potentate made us grovel, blubber, howl, and shudder; no indignity was too extreme if it broke down our defenses. After I left the class, it was rumored that one of his students had to be wheeled off to Bellevue in a buttonless jacket with wraparound sleeves.

The time, energy, and money it takes to promote thirty seconds of Nike or sixty seconds of Sprite probably exceeds the gross national product of half a dozen countries. The more time I spent with Hannah Lee, the more appalled I became by my so-called life.

An independent filmmaker friend of mine met Hannah Lee and me for tea one afternoon after Hannah's appointment with her New York doctors. Jim was smitten with Hannah and, afterward, wanted all the details we hadn't covered in our nonstop two-hour get-together. Would she, he wondered, ever be interested in shooting a documentary that chronicled one day in her life?

Hannah had often said she wanted to share her story with a broader audience, in part because she felt most people were ill informed about diabetes, in part because she was a natural communicator, and in largest part because she had never seen anything on film about death and dying, anything, that is, that she felt was realistic. I remember laughing with her about the classic deathbed scenes in *Gone With the Wind* and *Little Women,* where Melanie and Beth, respectively, seemed to be visited by the vapors instead of the Grim Reaper. The early "talkies" were even sillier; many of the film stars of the day subscribed to the Delsarte style of acting, where a simple wrist to the forehead telegraphed the heroine's dire straits to her nail-biting audience.

After Jim and I had several extended visits with Hannah and her family—in particular, with her mother and her aunt, two liberal septuagenarians—plans for a documentary were under way.

Jim lined up a crew and a postproduction facility as I backed into the producer-interviewer role, not realizing at the time that my acting days were numbered.

One of the most touching scenes in the film took place between Hannah and a young, gay technician whom Hannah said she preferred over all the others for his gentleness, the kindly way he spoke to her, and the time he took to insert her dialysis needles—which was a very painful procedure twenty years ago. On camera, as he began to hook her up to the giant mechanical blood-cleaner, I asked both of them what it was that bound them together.

"He cares," she said. "He really cares."

He looked at her shyly and said, "Oh, Hannah, I was just going to say the same thing about you."

The intimacy and the magnitude of living with dying—of learning more about Hannah's most private thoughts and feelings, of asking questions to her fellow patients in a dialysis unit as well as to her family, friends, and doctors, of working into the night with a crew who had already donated their services and who, in the end, were moved to tears by Hannah Lee's courage and perseverance—made me wonder how in the world I could possibly continue to pitch Procter & Gamble products to an ambivalent public.

Hannah Lee told us that the experience had changed her life, but there was also no question that it had changed ours. Perhaps the story of a nine-year-old Hannah best captures her spirit and its effect on all of us. It was then, when diagnosed with diabetes, that Hannah asked her mother on the way home from Boston's Joslin Clinic, "Why me, Mom? Why me?"

Her mother, groping for a response, told her the following: "There is something called the Law of Compensation that says for every loss there is a gain."

"I felt like a damn fool at the time," her mother said, "telling that to a nine-year-old. But I felt I had to say something. And you know, since childhood, Hannah Lee always had a genuine interest in people. She was sensitive to their needs . . . truly cared about them, about their problems. She was a devoted friend . . . called, wrote, always so supportive . . . I do think, in spite of her difficulties, Hannah gained something beyond measure. I think we all did."

Hannah Lee died a year after the filming. Neither she nor we ever saw a final version of the documentary—it was deemed "too depressing" by top brass and scuttled midstream—but she did take part in our initial meetings and worked on the rough cut with a gentle man named Fred Flamenhaft, who was an NBC staff producer. They were instantaneous friends, a result, I believe, of their mutual vulnerability. Fred, who had a brain tumor, died a year and a half after Hannah Lee.

At what point and for how long our lives intersect is far less important than what transpires when they do. The few hours that Hannah Lee and Fred spent together constituted a lifetime of understanding. To this day I like to envision them collaborating on a whole series of heavenly projects more far-reaching than any of us could ever imagine, each one completely underwritten and commercial-free.

Hannah Lee Beck altered the course of my life. If it weren't for her, I wouldn't have met or worked with many of the people who have since become my friends. Sometimes I feel Hannah sitting on my shoulder, whispering in my ear— You have loved, given birth; you have lived to see the seasons change.

So off they went together. But wherever they go, and whatever happens to them on the way, in that enchanted place in the top of the Forest, a little boy and his Bear will always be playing.

—A. A. MILNE

ELEVEN

Children

Curiosity underscores every stage of life. Without it we would be a pretty dull bunch. Yet when it comes to death and grief, even the most curious among us clam up.

Carl Jung believed that "the negation of life's fulfillment is synonymous with the refusal to accept its ending. Not wanting to die," he wrote, "is identical with not wanting to live." In *The Healing Heart,* Norman Cousins concludes that "death is not the enemy; living in constant fear of it is." How can the rest of us become more accepting of their wise conclusions?

Perhaps, quite simply, by listening to our children.

Recently, I met a woman whose husband had died several years ago, just days after his fortieth birthday. Betsy said she and her husband had been "soul mates" from the moment they met until his death ten years later. They could communicate almost, she said, "without talking." And so it did not seem at all strange for her, as he lay dying of a brain tumor in the bedroom of their home, to curl up beside him "in spoon position," as was their habit, and ask him to give her a sign.

"You mean after I am dead?" he asked, his voice, a whisper.

"Yes," she said, "so I know that you're safe."

"But what if I can't? What if I'm not able to?"

"You'll be able to," she said. "I just have to believe you will."

He died a week later. After his body had been taken away, Betsy's two-year-old son came into their bedroom with her father, who was quite close to the little boy. This was a child who, Betsy said, "was an observer, a child who, save a word here and there, barely talked at all."

Suddenly, Betsy remembered, her son "stretched his arms up toward the section of the ceiling over the bed, and said, 'Daddy, Daddy, hold me, hold me.' It was incredible. He had never, ever put words together like that before or spoken so clearly. My father, a no-nonsense surgeon, was speechless. It was obvious to both of us that my husband was present in some form and my son could see him, even if we couldn't."

Betsy described waking up in the middle of the night two weeks later and feeling "absolutely" that her husband was there, first as a "kind of energy" surging through the the room, and then in a calmer form, tucked in beside her in the very configuration they had always slept in.

"He was there by my side for—I'm not sure how long, really—but I experienced an amazing sense of peace and well-being. It was the sign I had hoped for."

———

Betsy has told very few people about these experiences; like the bank teller, she fears they might think she is crazy, a refrain that I have heard too many times to count. Yet I believe if we grant ourselves a grace period to observe and to listen, we might learn a few things, one being that at our most basic, we too are sensate creatures.

Small children remind us of this every day. They help us to strip away the pretense, to see and respond in a more open way, as Betsy's son did, without a smidgen of self-consciousness.

Elisabeth Kübler-Ross has said that dying children often express their feelings more naturally than adults. Terminally ill children often speak of their dreams and visions, according to pediatric oncologist Diane Komp, the author of *A Child Shall Lead Them* and *A Window to Heaven*. She writes, "For adults, the so called 'near-death experience' is often spiritually *revolutionary*, a type of conversion experience that puts them on a new road. For children, however, the experience is more spiritually *evolutionary*, progress on an already familiar pathway."

My friend Cathy, a teacher and a painter, is one of those rare grown-ups who both understands and speaks the language of children. Last year when her husband, George, who had just turned seventy, died suddenly, their large Greek family, along with their extended family of friends and neighbors, rallied around.

As people waited in a long line that stretched out of the

funeral home into the December night, Cathy took time to greet every person, frequently breaking into tears as she listened to their memories of George. After watching this from a corner of the room, Cathy's six-year-old granddaughter, Alexandra, approached her tentatively.

"Yaya," she asked, "why do you cry every time a new person talks to you?"

"Because I am sad about Papou," Cathy said, "but when I look into your face, it makes me happy again." After that, for the rest of the evening, when Cathy began to cry, her granddaughter would sidle up, slip one finger into her Yaya's hand and present a beaming countenance front and center.

George and Cathy—Papou and Yaya to their grandchildren—had known each other since childhood. George, who had been a devout member of the Greek Orthodox faith until the day he died, had told Cathy he wanted a traditional service, one that would require, among other things, an open casket. Knowing that this might frighten her grandchildren, Cathy walked them through the details the morning of George's funeral. Little Georgie, her four-year-old grandson, listened soberly as Cathy explained that they would be seeing Papou the next day but that even though his body was there, Papou had died and had gone to heaven with the angels.

Sitting cross-legged on the floor, fiddling with his shoelaces, Georgie tried to make sense of what his Yaya had just told him. Suddenly he brightened, looked up at Cathy, and said, "Oh, *I* get it, Yaya . . . you mean Papou is *there* . . . he's just not *in*."

Cathy remembers an incident that occurred two months before George's death that she thinks of now as the children's "preparation." On a warm autumn day she and Alexandra and Georgie, who visited their grandparents at least twice a week, were painting self-portraits at the kitchen table when a wren crashed into the plate-glass door behind them and fell to the ground with a broken neck. The children were so distraught that Cathy suggested they create a special ritual and bury the little bird in the backyard. Georgie and Alex went off to retrieve a shoe box from the back of their Yaya's closet and then proceeded to paint it with the bright acrylic colors they had been using. After setting the newly painted box and lid to dry in the sun on the patio, the children searched for "favorite birdie things." They collected enough grass and acorns and yellow mums to feather the deceased's final nesting place. After digging a hole with Papou's shovel, each child gave a blessing.

"I want to hug you and I'll always miss you, birdie," said Georgie.

"Birdie, I wish you could stay alive. We made you a nice home while you are dead. I hope you love it," said Alex.

Then they solemnly placed the box in the ground and began to cover it with handfuls of earth.

"Wait a minute!" cried Alexandra, "what about the birdie's parents? They will be looking for him."

"Why don't you write them a letter and tell them what happened," Cathy suggested.

After much deliberation, Georgie and Alexandra came up with the following message and tacked it to the maple tree that shaded the small grave with its spindly twig cross:

> Your birdie is dead, but we
> put it in a nice box and buried it.
> Don't worry. He's in heaven
> with our dogs, Nikki and Kato.
>   Love, Alex and Georgie

Nothing more to add here save the words of Henri Frederic Amiel:

> Blessed be childhood, which brings down something
> of heaven into the midst of our rough earthliness.

House Lights Down

In the straight-back wooden chairs of eternity left
from a recent run of Our Town, *I sit beside you*
to tell the darkness how we endure endless forfeiture,
how our days disappear, how all we do must be left
undone. As on a pocket watch that never opens face,
the unregarded hours elude us and convey seconds

into seasons, making a surrealism of years. Already we have
not walked far enough in snow, swum deep enough into the lake.
We haven't read a week of Keats or memorized seven
minutes of Mahler. Will we ever pick a wild peach, step
on shadows in Sicily or stones in the Bering Sea?
All unlikely. Like bees abandoning an autumn field,

we yield, relinquishing our nightclothes and notebooks, the lost
powdery scent of our missing infant, the dazzling waltz,
the daily bread and the best words, left unsaid. Ours is this
small space between an answered prayer and a coming
curse. Still, we are honored to have played our part, lovers
living our days unrehearsed, as if each were the first.

—SUSAN KINSOLVING

TWELVE

Macaroni and Butterflies

On my mother's third day in hospice a woman in a crisp pink apron maneuvered an aluminum cart on wheels—three shelves of colored paper, spools of thread, tubes of glue, and plastic cylinders of felt-tipped markers, scissors, pipe cleaners, paints, brushes, crayons and beads—and stopped it just short of my mother's bed.

"Would you like to make a card today?" she said, holding up an already finished example as artistic enticement.

"No, I don't think so," I said, "thanks."

"Crafts can be very theraputic." She nodded at the bed diagonally across from us where a young woman visiting her grandfather was making concentric circles with Elmer's Glue on a square of red construction paper. "It's collage day. Glitter, buttons, macaroni—whatever you'd like to use."

"No, really, thanks."

"It may make you feel better."

"Look, I appreciate your effort," I said, "I just don't think it's my medium."

"Well, alright," she said. "You're sure now?"

"I'm sure."

As she started to wheel off, she looked up and spotted the wide strip of corkboard suspended over the foot of the bed and festooned with leaves and vines from the woods near our house—the last of the fall foliage my mother so loved—that I had pinned up the day before.

"Oh, how nice. Did you do that?"

"Yes."

"Very imaginative."

"Thanks. It looked better yesterday. The leaves are beginning to dry out now," I said ruefully, already dreading its deconstruction at day's end.

An hour later, Kathy, my favorite nurse on the west wing, came by and pointed to the corkboard. "Word's out you're angling for the position of creative director."

"Gimme a break."

"No, really," she said, laughing, "we could use you around here."

My mother would have adored Kathy. Direct gaze, quick wit, merry face . . . that Celtic connection that instantly said home to both of us. The minute I met Kathy, I felt she was meant to be our guide.

"How long have you worked here?" I had asked on that first day.

"Ten years."

"Long time."

"Mmm."

"How's that been?"

"People always ask if I get depressed. It's hard to explain, but after two days off, I can't wait to get back to hospice. To tell you the truth, I can't imagine doing anything else."

Kathy's dream for the future is to open her own hospice, where every room has a view of the sea and every bed has cotton sheets and comforters.

"It's the way I'd like to be treated when I'm dying," she says.

Kathy and the other nurses often use this grounding reminder as they counsel families. Momentary role reversal. Imagining one's own death dispels ambiguity. What will give comfort? Who will be there? How will we respond? Were I to die tomorrow, one thing I know for sure: no posers—as my daughter calls them—allowed.

With this in mind, I limited my mother's visitors to people who really knew and loved her. In those final days there was enough emotional strain without the addition of people who "wanted to pay their respects" but had had little contact with my mother in the last years of her life. It's amazing how some people seem to vaporize with the onset of serious illness, but I suppose it's a good litmus test for loyalty. In sickness and in health, for better or for worse, till death do us part, are tribal prerequisites. When the tribe showed up, I encouraged them to talk to my mother as they always had, using the same tone, the same humor, the same well-worn stories.

Initially my daughter, who had just turned fourteen, was hesitant about "saying the right thing to Nana."

"There's no right or wrong, only true," I said. "Be yourself. Why don't you talk about the things you did together? Remember the story about the watch, or 'Pippa Mouse'? Or the penny jar? She'll hear you, I'm sure of it."

". . . maybe I'll tell her to say hi to Grandpa Ted."

"See? You know exactly what to say."

And she did. Just a few weeks ago, before the second anniversary of my mother's death (most of us know instinctively when these anniversaries occur, even though we may not mark them), my daughter followed me into the kitchen after dinner.

"I had a dream about Nana last night, Mom, and she looked really good . . . she was laughing . . . we were laughing together . . . eating grilled cheese sandwiches . . . she wasn't sick anymore. It got me thinking . . . I'm glad I was able to . . . to say goodbye. I feel like I said everything I needed to say to her."

My daughter's words swept aside, at least momentarily, all maternal self-doubts, those ubiquitous should-haves and could-haves of parenthood. On this issue, my teenager and I were in hormone-free harmony. Because she had trusted me and then in turn had trusted herself, we now have the reassurance that my mother did not die alone, that we were there to let her know how much she meant to us, each in our own way. The bond between mother and daughter was strengthened by this experience, as was the spiritual bridge that continues to connect us to my mother.

Spiritual connections are as likely to precede death as to follow it. Many people hear voices or see faces, as my mother and Elaine did, or speak to long-deceased relatives, saying things like "I'm coming with you," "Wait for me," or "I'm going home now." Hospice workers say these occurrences are quite common, and they encourage families to follow the lead of those who are dying, rather than impose their own ideas of a perfect death.

Take, for example, Susan, a friend of a friend, who had converted to Buddhism from Catholicism when she was in her twenties. Years later, as her father lay dying in the Santa Rosa ranch house where she had grown up, Susan moved home to nurse him through his last weeks of life. Over time she draped colorful shawls around his bedroom, set up several altars and filled them with fetishes, incense, beads, and candles, played recordings of chanting monks, and read aloud to him daily from *The Tibetan Book of the Dead*. After a week of this, Susan's semicomatose father managed to open one eye and say, "Don't you think you're overdoing it a little, Susan?"

The doctors in a New York hospital told my friend Connie that her father, who suffered from end-stage colon cancer, had only hours to live. Two weeks later, medical prescience notwithstanding, the grieving family still surrounded his bedside, strung out and unsure what to do. After a family huddle, Connie, a psychotherapist and the family spokesperson, decided to whisper words of encouragement in her father's ear. "Daddy," she said, "it's okay to die. Follow the love. Go toward the light." Suddenly her father, who was German-born, opened his eyes, lifted his head off the pillow, and glared at her. "I vill not!" he boomed. Shaken, though heartened by the return of his characteristic stubbornness, the family decided to go home and get some rest. He died later that evening.

My friend Mark recently told me about his last visits with his father, who was dying of congestive heart failure in the family's summer home in Truro on Cape Cod. A painter and a sculptor who worked in his studio until three days before he died, Mark's "self-involved" father rarely, if ever, praised his own artistically talented children, a fact that makes his son's last memories of him all the more meaningful.

A few weeks before his death, as the two of them sat on the deck looking out over the marshes, Mark's father suddenly and uncharacteristically said, "There is so much goodness in the world," paused for a moment, and then repeated it.

Mark, an architect who flew between his work in Connecticut and the Cape every week, said that on one of his last visits, as he entered the room, his father looked up and lovingly exclaimed, "Shana boychik, shana boychik," which in Yiddish means "beautiful boy." Although his father, the son of Eastern

European immigrants, had grown up speaking this language, Mark had never ever heard him utter a word of it. Later that day, when Mark showed him photographs of a house he had designed in a national magazine, his father carefully traced and retraced with a shaky hand the roof brackets and the windows which, as Mark said, "danced against each other in different rhythms," and finally gave his son the thumbs-up sign, an indication to Mark that his father had not only "recognized the complexity of the relationship between the two elements" but was quite proud of him as well.

Mark says this time with his father was "a powerful affirmation."

Affirmations come and go, in a variety of forms, at the end of life. In a sense, it is a time for the dying to "take their moment" and whether their feelings are spoken or unspoken, it is the time for the living to pay very close attention. Hospice workers say that hearing is the last sense to go. The tricky part for the living is learning to "listen" when nothing is being said, to speak even though it "appears" that they are not being heard, to respond to nuance, to tread lightly on unfamiliar ground, even though the footing feels tenuous.

When my Aunt Marie arrived on my mother's seventh day in hospice, she was shocked to see her only sibling, eleven years her senior, curled in the fetal position beneath the covers, physically wasted, eyes half closed, mouth half open, suspended somewhere between this world and the next.

"I told her you were coming," I said. "I think she's been waiting. Do you want to talk to her?"

"Do you really think she can hear me?" Marie asked.

"I do."

With that, Marie was at my mother's side, stroking her hair, revisiting memories from their life together before husbands and children, memories of hand-me-down skates and Girl Scout socks, of Aunt Lizzie's malapropisms and lunches at Schrafft's. She sang "Falling in Love with Love"—I had forgotten it was my mother's favorite—and quoted from memory a part of a Yeats poem they both loved:

When you are old and gray and full of sleep,
And nodding by the fire, take down this book,
And slowly read, and dream of the soft look
Your eyes had once, and of their shadows deep;
How many loved your moments of glad grace,
And loved your beauty with love false or true . . .

Suddenly my mother's lips began to move, as if she were trying to talk. Marie and I stared at each other, electrified by her response. I whispered in my mother's ear that I could see she wanted to speak, but she didn't have to if it was too much of a strain; we knew she could hear us; we knew she loved us as we loved her.

"I'm so glad you waited for me, Helen," Marie said, caressing my mother's arm. I was touched by my aunt's spontaneity, by her complete and unself-conscious immersion in this moment, a moment she would later refer to as "our circle of three, behind the drawn curtain around your mother's bed as if we were in a cocoon, totally removed from the rest of the world . . . I felt the vibrations going from you to Helen to me . . . almost like a trinity."

We continued our vigil for forty-eight hours—at my mother's bedside, over lunch in a nearby restaurant, at home before going to bed, in the car to and from hospice. We remembered and celebrated, just the two of us—my husband was out of town and my daughter had gone to a friend's house for the weekend—each sparking the other's memories and sometimes uncovering new ones; laughing and crying and tapping into our nutty family archive, allied in what we now both consider to be one of the most profound and transcendent experiences of our lives. We will be forever united in our memories of this elegiac time, dragging out our panoply of long-dormant "Helen stories": the time she came to Thanksgiving dinner dressed as (early) Madonna, laden in rhinestones and lace; the time she locked my father out of their hotel room after a fight and he wandered the halls in his raincoat until Marie and her husband took him in; the time, clad in a new Black-watch plaid kilt, she broke into a ridiculous rendition of an Irish step dance until Marie and their mother were "laughing until they cried." My mother's was a family of funny women.

My grandmother had two sisters and two daughters; my mother had one daughter; Marie had four; and her daughters, my cousins, and I have four between us. All girls. As far back as I can remember, self-deprecation and nonstop hilarity defined every family reunion. No one ever finished a sentence, which was perfectly natural to my mother, who considered "constant interruption the key to a lively conversation."

Marie and I continued *our* conversation with Kathy when she came by at the end of her shift. We recounted how my mother had tried to talk earlier in the day. Kathy nodded. What seems miraculous in the "outside world" often is run-of-the-mill at hospice, a place where the ordinary overlaps with the sacred every day. In hospice, living with dying seems to foster a more down-to-earth approach to spirituality—a comfort, no doubt, to the growing number of aging baby boomers, like myself, whose religious boundaries, smudged during the sixties, are now up for midlife review.

My mother was a long-lapsed Catholic; my father, a primary Episcopalian, a secondary Presbyterian, and, until he and his brothers were caught sailing collection plates from the choir loft, an occasional Methodist. In spite of my parents' Christmas-and-Easter-only appearances, I was baptized and confirmed in the Episcopal Church. I learned to love the hymns, the psalms, and the added special events. My favorites included vichyssoise at the Duquesne Club with Mrs. McCaskey's Sunday school class before *Ben Hur,* and chocolate-covered strawberries at the annual spring festival under a green-and-white-striped tent. As I told Kathy, except for the *Ben Hur* part, suburban Episcopalianism was hardly the ideal preparation for death.

"Hey, that's nothing," Kathy said. "My mother was a complete atheist. She used to say, 'When you're dead, you're dead. That's it. The end. *Finito.*' My mother didn't have a spiritual bone in her body."

I asked Kathy if she had met other people like that during her time in hospice.

"Ed." She smiled. "We still talk about Ed."

It seems Ed had arrived at hospice in the last stages of metastatic cancer with no family, no insurance, and no hope. He was depressed and uncommunicative. But the day after he was admitted, one of the volunteers took it upon herself to organize treatments for Ed. She convinced a nearby hospital to provide radiation therapy and then coordinated a group of people to drive him to and from his appointments. Ed was so moved by this volunteer effort that, as Kathy put it, he relaxed. He opened up. He began to interact with the staff and the volunteers. And so, Kathy said, she was not at all surprised when she came to say good night to Ed two weeks into his stay and he "sat bolt upright in bed and said, 'I am finally happy' and died in the next moment with an incredible smile on his face." Kathy paused. "That really made me a believer. That, and the butterflies."

"Butterflies?" I asked.

"After my mother died, I would head for the beach every Sunday. It was the only place I could be alone, the only place I could let down and cry. Then I began to notice that every time I thought about my mother, butterflies would cluster around me. It was the oddest thing. As the kids got older, whenever a butterfly came close, I'd say, 'There's grandma, she's hanging around again.' It got to be a kind of family joke.

"Another time I was sitting in the garden at hospice on a bench under the wisteria arbor waiting for my husband and kids to pick me up after work when Miriam, a woman who worked at hospice and really reminded me of my mother, came toward me with this incredulous look on her face.

" 'Kathy,' she said, 'don't move. You won't believe it, but there is a great big monarch butterfly on your head.'

" 'Oh, I believe it, Miriam,' I said. 'That's my mother.'

The butterfly lingered and finally fluttered off as Kathy explained her beach walks to Miriam. When she finished the story, the butterfly returned, landed on the very same spot on Kathy's head, and stayed long past the point of coincidence.

Kathy tells this story over and over again, most often to children whose parents are dying.

"There's more to this than any of us can imagine," she tells them. "Just because you can't see your mother or touch your mother doesn't mean you can't communicate with her." As that belief has been an ongoing comfort for Kathy, she hopes it will be for these children as well. "We're all in this together," she says, which could well be the hospice creed.

Elaine's oldest son, Pedro, following in the artistic footsteps of his parents, has become a sculptor. His elegant kinetic works, crafted from stainless steel, aluminum, and mahogany, have a surprising lightness, their fine-tuned movements set in motion by a whisper of air or the touch of a finger.

Just before Elaine died, Pedro completed a piece he decided at the last minute to call *Butterfly*. He dedicated it to his mother. The surprising connection between this sculpture and Elaine's arm movements two months later, which Pedro recalls were "as delicate as a butterfly's," was reinforced yet again the morning after her death. When the people from the funeral home arrived, the family requested that they place Elaine's body beside the stone cairn for a brief time before taking her away. Pedro said no sooner had they done this than a late-in-the-season butterfly appeared, hovered over the cairn, and then circled around and around Elaine. The butterfly visitations did not end there. One year later, as Elaine's daughter Tessa prepared to mix her mother's ashes into the newly poured concrete foundation of the house she and her husband were building with friends and family, another butterfly appeared "out of nowhere" and flew under Tessa's outstretched arms and around the spot where Elaine's ashes were to be scattered.

———————

Walk into any hospice in any part of the world and it is guaran-
teed you will hear a butterfly story. In fact, last week marked
the twenty-fifth birthday of Connecticut Hospice, the first
hospice in America, founded in 1974 by a group of New
Haven–area nurses, doctors, and clergy. A commemorative
postage stamp honoring their work was unveiled at a ceremony
at Yale Divinity School, a stamp that features a white pathway
curving up a green lawn to a two-story house with a purple
roof. Overhead a golden butterfly twice the size of the house
hovers like a celestial helicopter. If the U.S. Postal Service can
okay an image like this, there's got to be hope for the world.
Think of it. That little square flying around the globe, affixed
to envelopes large and small, a modern-day nod to an ancient
Greek belief. In their language, the word for "butterfly" and
"soul" was one and the same.

Death is different from what anyone knows, and luckier.

—WALT WHITMAN

THIRTEEN

Creature Comforts

Here's one thing I've discovered while writing this book. Tell a story about butterflies and you'll hear one about flowers.

Our friend Julia has lived the last forty-two of her eighty-seven years in a large house on the outskirts of Boston. Two summers ago, a week after the death of her ninety-two-year-old husband, Paul, Julia noticed that the wisteria vine he had nurtured and trained to grow along the picket fence in their front yard was loaded with purple blossoms. This would not be unusual except for the fact that Paul, an experienced gardener, had been trying in vain to get this stubborn vine to flower since 1956. That's 1956. Though not particularly spiritual or sentimental, Julia, a member of the Neptune Society ("for six hundred dollars they take care of things after I die") says she absolutely believes Paul "looked down from above, pointed his finger at the wisteria, and commanded it to *bloom*. And," as Julia says, "it most certainly did."

When I heard Julia's story, it reminded me of one I had heard as a teenager when a dear friend of my parents died suddenly in his sleep. After the funeral his wife, Jane, took my mother aside and confided that their ten-year-old spider plant, which had never before flowered, bore two perfect white blossoms the morning after her husband's death. At the time I thought it was a charming oddity, but I have since come to believe, as Jane obviously did, that it was a "sign" from her husband.

Flowers begat bug stories.

Last May, at my friend Michael's fiftieth-birthday party, his mother-in-law, Shirley, with whom he had been very close, made an appearance in the form of a luna moth, or so believes his wife. However, their daughter Amy, a just-the-facts-ma'am AP reporter, challenged her mother's assumption.

"Why would Gram have chosen a moth, Mom? She hated bugs. You know that."

"Well," her mother replied, "maybe it was the only ride she could get."

Gail, one of Elaine's closest friends, told me that the morning after Elaine died, a praying mantis alighted on the floor of the back deck where her family had gathered in the Indian summer sun to remember and mourn their dear friend's passing. After a time everyone except Gail went into the house. As she sat quietly thinking about Elaine, the mantis "suddenly flew up to the back of the empty chair, faced [her] and remained there, eye to eye, for a very long time."

Gail also told me that right after the death of her mother-

in-law, who was constantly knitting or crocheting, a big black spider spun an intricate web across the top half of their front door.

Bugs have led to birds. To date, I've collected stories about an English robin, a bluebird, a seagull, a cardinal, a humming-bird, a red-tailed hawk, and a great blue heron. Please forgive me, but in order to convince you of each story's importance, I've decided to tell them all:

1. When Jean's parents retired to the Welsh countryside, her father cultivated a thriving garden. Every spring as he tilled the soil in preparation for planting, an English robin would appear and sit on the fence that bordered his plot.

"We got to calling him the house robin because he was always around. Sometimes he would even sit on Daddy's shoulder," Jean remembers. "English robins are smaller than yours, more aggressive and territorial, and often come back to the same place year after year."

One spring Jean's father fell ill and was rushed to the hospital, where he died three days later. On the afternoon of his death, Jean went home and opened his bedroom window with the garden view to let in some fresh air. No sooner had she done this than the robin—her father's robin—flew into the room and perched on the headboard of his bed and "stayed for a very long time."

2. Emily's mother died of a heart aneurysm when she was fifty-four. A shy woman who loved the outdoors, she had once

told her children that if there were such a thing as reincarnation, she would like to come back as a bluebird. Wanting a retreat from the Chicago suburb where Emily and her siblings grew up, their mother designed and built a small stone house on Wisconsin's Door County peninsula, modeled after the cottages she had admired in Ireland. As a finishing touch, she hung a wooden house in a tree outside the kitchen window with hopes that a bluebird family would take up residence. She died two years later. A month after their mother's death Emily and her sister Kitty returned to the cottage to spend a weekend. When they awoke on Saturday morning, a bluebird was sitting on the outside ledge of their bedroom window, looking in. Twenty years later, when Emily was in the midst of her own family crisis, she went into the sunroom on the far side of her house to find a "window, mysteriously open, and a bluebird sitting high up on a drapery rod."

3. Pat's father was a lifelong sailor, or, as she calls him, an old sea dog. The day after he died, her mother opened the door of their home in rural Massachusetts, which was many miles inland, and was startled when a sea gull flew toward her and landed "not five feet from the front stoop."

4. Cathy's husband was a devoted alumnus of his alma mater, Wesleyan University. Two weeks after his death, Cathy returned from a friend's house to discover a pair of cardinals at the end of her driveway. It was January. As she drove up the long stretch of gravel, the cardinals seemed to fly just slightly

ahead of the car all the way to the top. Cathy always smiles when she tells this story, not because the birds were there in the dead of winter but because the cardinal is Wesleyan's mascot.

5. As Madelyn's mother lay dying of cancer, she told her daughter she would try to come back as a bird to let her know that she was alright. After her mother's death Madelyn told her sister, "*Something* happened but it certainly wasn't a sign." As she and a friend shared a brown bag lunch on a park bench, a hummingbird appeared, hovering at eye level. Madelyn was positive their mother "wouldn't have chosen such a bird, for it seemed hardly a bird at all." Astonished, Madelyn's sister described the gift she had hung by their mother's bedside a week before she died, which Madelyn, too overcome with grief, hadn't noticed: a tiny glass hummingbird no bigger than a thimble.

6. When Jeffrey, a twenty-eight-year-old dancer with AIDS, was close to death, his partner, Nelson, called several members of the Paul Taylor Dance Company in New York to tell them that it was time.

Two days after his death, dancers, friends, and family joined hands around the red-barked cherry tree planted on a favorite part of their land in Jeffrey's honor, his ashes now incorporated with the soil around its roots. In the midst of the memorial prayers and remembrances, a red-tailed hawk suddenly appeared. Flying uncharacteristically low, it circled the gathering three times. Hawks, though territorial, are known for keeping their distance, particularly from people. This makes it all the more astounding that a week after the memorial service, as Nelson was collecting mail from the battered box that bore his and Jeffrey's names, a hawk, the same red-tail, reappeared, landing four feet from where Nelson stood. Each one, human and bird, remained still, eyes locked. Nelson told me that this was a gift from Jeffrey, a reassurance he was safe and at peace. Nelson explained that Native Americans believe the hawk to be the most sacred of birds, the reembodiment of the spirit, a blessing above all blessings.

7. Nancy and Roy lived in an apartment on the top floor of a Victorian house in Haight-Ashbury. Their landlady, Bambi, a stout woman in her sixties who had once run the Basque Hotel in North Beach, lived in the ground-floor apartment and faithfully tended its small back garden. One of the more recognizable characters in the Panhandle, Bambi resembled a leather-clad stevedore as she roared around town on her motorcycle. But one day, heading out for an afternoon ride with helmet in hand, Bambi had a fatal heart attack.

The day after her funeral, as Nancy stood looking out their third-floor window at Bambi's small garden below, a great blue heron swooped down and landed in the minuscule, ankle-deep fishpond. The heron stood Kabukilike, turning its elegant head from side to side, splendidly regal. It was later conjectured that the heron was perhaps the reembodiment of

Bambi, a svelte alter ego, surveying her former venue, tongue-in-beak.

So . . . that's the skinny on the critters. Frankly, I'm surprised these stories came my way at all. It's really not my beat. I'm a pagan, not a vegan. I wear high heels, I eat red meat, and suede is a staple in my wardrobe. But frankly, when a spectrum of regular folks experience stuff like this, one can't help but think, Something's going on here—a something even *I* have to admit I've experienced firsthand in my own neck of the woods.

Our house is located on a lake that borders seven hundred acres of a land trust about the size of Central Park. Much as I miss the city, this place has a bounty of wildlife that almost makes up for the winter months when, for my own protection, I hide all the sharp objects in our house.

Our closest neighbors have feathers and fur, paws and wings. I've seen lake otters, deer, possums, raccoons, badgers, Canada geese, ospreys, kingfishers, herons, egrets, ducks, finches, jays, wrens, woodpeckers, and—for the first time ever last *February,* huddled together amid the frozen branches and shriveled berries of our weeping crabapple—six fat bluebirds. *Bluebirds.* I stood there, stunned, sponge in one hand, plate in the other, jaw practically dropped down the sink trap, mesmerized by this psychedelic blast of cerulean blue, the Audubon version of—what?—*Touched by an Angel?* Touched in the Head by an Angel? What do you do with this kind of information? Call Roger Tory Peterson? "Ripley's Believe It or Not"? Dismiss it as magical thinking and get on with the dishes? Of course not. You tell one last story to bolster the hallowed event.

Three chapters into this book I hit a patch of procrastination as I was writing about my mother's death. So I did what I do when I'm feeling sad or stuck: I headed for the woods to sit on the rock at the head of Iron Creek, which feeds our lake and looks exactly like those Sierra Club photographs of moss-covered boulders, tumbling water, and trees that reach the sky. This is my sanctuary. I come here to pray. I came here with my husband and daughter to scatter the first of my mother's ashes on Christmas morning two years ago. On this day I am lulled by the wind in the pines and the sensual pull of the earth. I bow my head. I think of my mother. I ask her for guidance. But I can't seem to focus. I open my eyes. I look up. And then I see it: an enormous hawk, soaring thirty yards downstream over a spot the local kids call Paradise Pool. Must be an osprey. Can't be a hawk. I never see hawks. She is flying upstream, headed in my direction. She is above me now, floating and circling. And then I see it. Her V-shaped, rose-feathered fan splinters the sunlight. I blink back the tears. I watch her in awe. In one crystalline instant, I become a believer.

Later that day I revisit a favorite passage from "The Prelude," by William Wordsworth.

Ah! need I say, dear friend! that to the brim
My heart was full; I made no vows, but vows
Were then made for me; bond unknown to me
Was given, that I should be, else sinning greatly,
A dedicated Spirit. On I walked
In thankful blessedness, which yet survives.

Be at peace with God, whatever you conceive Him to be, and whatever your labors and aspirations, in the noisy confusion of life, keep peace with your soul. With all its sham, drudgery and broken dreams, it is still a beautiful world. Be careful. Strive to be happy.

—"DESIDERATA"

FOURTEEN

Radical Departures

Because I didn't come into the world until five years after my parents married, I often wonder if their New York years were as turbulent as those of my childhood in Pittsburgh. Even now I can picture them leaving the house, smiling and resplendent, en route to some gala, and returning, hours later, in a Vesuvian fury.

Standing at the top of the stairway trembling—hands crossed over my chest as if to keep my heart from bursting out of my body and thumping down the steps—I would listen for the first sound: the distorted voices or the slammed door, the rare reprieve of laughter. Each, my cue to intervene or go back to bed. Hardly a month would go by without some drama igniting and burning out of control, the underlying sensuality apparent only now in retrospect. What bound them together— rage or libido or some combination of the two fueling each other—remains unclear. In that sense, I am still standing at the top of the stairs, listening.

After particularly wrenching skirmishes I remember them scooping me up in a three-way hug, dancing me around the room and singing "Little Brown Jug." I never knew what the little brown jug was, but I often envisioned a small glazed urn that held our joy in the midst of their wrath, keeping it safe until the storm had passed.

After my father died, my mother and I would laugh and cry, remembering him. She would say, "I was crazy about the guy. He could be a bastard, but I'd give anything to have him back."

She talked about some of their adventures, as well as a host of the endearing and rotten things he had said to her over the years. Finally, almost reverently, she told me about the last time they were together as husband and wife: the morning of their thirty-eighth wedding anniversary. It had been a long time since they had been intimate, my mother said—he had become quite childlike and distracted as his memory faded—and yet, five days before my father took his own life, he made love to my mother. Twice. And I don't think she would mind my telling you this because, to her, it was a spiritual union.

"He was so vital," she said a few weeks after his death. "So present. I know now it was a farewell."

When I look through the navy blue leather-bound family album, I turn the pages looking for clues, retracing the years before I was born—they are there without me then, as I am here without them now—black-and-white photographs of my mother, a model, my father, an army officer, both of them at the Stork Club before they were married. She is twenty-three.

He is thirty-five. Film-star handsome, they gaze at each other adoringly; my father in a dress uniform, my mother in a black sheath and pearls, strains of Gershwin nearly audible in the background.

There are also several yellowed newspaper articles, the most moving of which, a UPI feature dated November 1943, begins this way:

> Air Service Command Headquarters, Somewhere in Italy—Major Edmund A. Cobb, former Cornell University football star, today held a citation that probably is unique in this or any other war—a public commendation delivered by the enlisted men of his command on the Italian battlefield.

Over half of my father's men had been killed in seven straight days of artillery and aerial bombardment. No one expected to survive the carnage. The document looks as if it were typed on an old Underwood and bears the signatures—thirty-one in black ink and five in blue pencil—of the surviving soldiers of the "Advanced Echelon of the III Air Service Area Command." I wonder if any of them are alive today. Pietro Simone, Joseph Leahy, Henry Jost, Frank Morris, Leo O'Brien, Robert Bloomfield, Leonard Ringle, Philip D'Agostino, Carmen Ashworth—just some of the thirty-six men who took it upon themselves to write this letter in the aftermath of battle. How I would love to hear their version of the story my father once told me—at my insistence and with great reluctance—a few years before his death. It was the one time in my life I saw my father cry. His tears, withheld for three decades, fell now for the many young men who had died in action.

He described the feelings of that day: being awakened by one of his lieutenants, rising, dressing hurriedly, emerging from his tent into the chill of a grey Sicilian dawn, rubbing his eyes and walking toward a ragtag band of soldiers standing in formation at attention, saluting my father. Puzzled, he returned their salute and listened to the following words:

> "We wish to commend Major Edmund Cobb for the great qualities of leadership he displayed as commanding officer of our detachment. Throughout the present campaign, Major Cobb never failed to inspire confidence in all personnel under his command. At one time, during the critical period of establishing the Salerno Beachhead, we were called upon to strengthen the second line of defense against an impending breakthrough. Before the detachment took up its position, Major Cobb delivered these inspiring words: "Remember, men, if we are called upon to fight, I want you to know I'll be right in front of you." From that moment on, the confidence of all the men was cemented to Major Cobb, and we feel that these words gave us the courage and strength to

pull through almost certain disaster. He is held in our highest esteem."

My father, it was reported, stood silently for a few seconds, saluted his command, and walked back to his quarters without a word.

"I couldn't speak," he told me through tears. "That was the finest thing that ever happened to a man."

My father never mentioned it again. My mother said, "I hope you tell his story someday."

Actually, I hadn't planned to. But this book about death has taken on a life of its own. The journey—full of twists and turns and strange unveilings—has been as much of a surprise as a meditation. I believe my parents and Elaine have been with me every step of the way—my trio of spirit guides, *my ghost writers* whose quiet but reassuring presence has convinced me that the next world may not be as hard to reach as most of us imagine.

Just last week my mother came to me in a dream. We were seated together at a small bistrolike table that held two glasses of wine, a basket of bread, and a blue ramekin of butter. Though draped in linen and traditionally set with flatware, our table was completely surrounded by water, a little island reserved for our own private reunion. We sat with our heads together, my mother and I, talking and laughing into the night, as if we had all the time in the world to rejoice in our good fortune.

These days, whether I'm dreaming or awake, it seems the more open I am, the more reinforcement I get. I have learned to pay better attention to the world around me and to be truer to my deepest instincts. I have learned that as much as I'm comforted by the woods, I need the sidewalks—and the people. Which is why I have finally decided—that is, my family and I have decided—to move back to New York City, the place I can once again, for now at least, call home.

I'll visit all my favorite haunts to celebrate our return: a quiet bench in the Conservatory Garden in spring, an early morning skate at Wollman Rink in winter, a summer performance at the Delacorte, the red-tailed hawks' nest on Fifth Avenue, a massage with Dora, the #6 line to Grand Central for a dozen Blue Points at the Oyster Bar, and a grateful stop at the Lady Chapel, where I'll light a candle, just in case.

Should you think this a radical departure from the country, I suggest you join me on a gentle slope in Central Park just a stone's throw from the Shakespeare Garden and Strawberry Fields, where, on summer weekends, a troubadour with a golden voice and the face of an angel stands by the lake and sings his stories to the people on the hill. They listen. They smile. They sing along. They must recognize, as I do, something in the guitar man's eyes that keeps them coming to this hill, something that speaks of loss and pain and renewal. It is a kind of benediction, really, a reassurance that we are able to emerge from suffering—and be changed.

ACKNOWLEDGMENTS

This book came to life because of two people's unwavering support and encouragement: Judith Jones, my friend at Knopf, and Dan Frank, my editor at Pantheon, believed in this project from its earliest days—I think of them, respectively and sometimes interchangeably, as my guardian angel and my guiding light.

Ellen Foley James has been a loyal friend who's seen me through several revolutions—personal as well as professional—and heads up a tribe I'm proud to call my own: Jayne Osgood, Connie Perelson, Pam Townshend, Rebecca Behrends, Caroline Officer Wharton, Susan Alper, Marianna Houston Weber, Missy Stevens, Carol Cooper Garey, Nicole Young, Larry Ashmead, Barbara Wherry Meyer, Catherine Prevert, Daniel Vogel, Elizabeth Zeschin, the extended families of Perelsons, de Movellans, Jameses, Langmuirs, and Townshends, as well as the craypas crew by the sea—Carol Anthony, Karen Silk, Ruth Miller, Cathy Frantzsis, and Elizabeth MacDonald. Bless them, one and all, for laughing and listening and hanging in.

The wonder women of Pantheon are in a category all their own, each brilliantly adept in their own corners of the twenty-fifth floor. Jennifer Weh—editorially and spiritually wise beyond her years—was a joy to work with, as were Sophie

Cottrell, Janice Goldklang, and Joy Dallanegra-Sanger, who seemed like old friends from that first lunch onward. In addition, I deeply appreciate the efforts of copy editor Fred Wiemer, designer Johanna Roebas, production editor Susan Norton, and managing editor Altie Karper, and the artistic contributions of Marge Anderson, Paul Langmuir, Archie Ferguson, and Lisa Hamilton.

Heartfelt thanks also go to: Marie Moorehead, Virginia Cobb, Marlee Brockman, Charles Boyd, Kathy Corbett and the women on the west wing of Connecticut Hospice, the Reverend Martin Montonye, Jenny McCobb at the Gables, Gail Reson, Pat Pratt, Jean Onesti, Julia Child, John Hamm, Mark Simon, Emily Foley, Ida and Jerry Franklin, Phoebe and Charley Dey, Molly Chappellet, Jeanette Horn, Ginger Junkin, Bunny Tavares, Linda Brandt, Anne Farrow, C.D.B. Bryan, Alice Mattison, Susan Kinsolving, Donald Hall, Nelson Bloncourt, Phyllis Joffee, Jonathan Dolger, David Budries, Mary and Carl Culberson, Rennie McQuilken, my friends at Alabaster and at Velvet da Vinci on Hayes Street in San Francisco, and the miraculous Fern Berman.

And finally, my gratitude and abiding love to the people who live with me in the woods—my husband Geoffrey Drummond and our daughter Leland—for the fabulous home-cooked meals and the nights spent dancing around the living room with our family of three.